CONNECTIVITY, THE ANSWER TO ENDING IGNORANCE AND SEPARATION

Can You Hear Me Yet?

Judy Breck

ScarecrowEducation
Lanham, Maryland • Toronto • Oxford
2004

Published in the United States of America
by ScarecrowEducation
An imprint of The Rowman & Littlefield Publishing Group, Inc.
4501 Forbes Boulevard, Suite 200, Lanham, Maryland 20706
www.scarecroweducation.com

PO Box 317
Oxford
OX2 9RU, UK

British Library Cataloguing in Publication Information Available

Library of Congress Cataloging-in-Publication Data

Breck, Judy, 1936–
Connectivity, the answer to ending ignorance and separation : can you hear me yet? / Judy Breck.
p. cm.
Includes bibliographical references and index.

ISBN: 978-1-57886-040-1

1. Internet in education. 2. Computer networks. 3. Education—Effect of technological innovations on. I. Title: Connectivity. II. Title: Answer to ending ignorance and separation. III. Title: Can you hear me yet?. IV. Title.
LB1044.87 .B724 2004
371.33′467′8—dc21 2003014565

∞™ The paper used in this publication meets the minimum requirements of American National Standard for Information Sciences—Permanence of Paper for Printed Library Materials, ANSI/NISO Z39.48-1992.
Manufactured in the United States of America.

For everyone we cannot hear yet.

CONTENTS

PREFACE

Like the up-close unfolding of evolution Charles Darwin encountered with the finches of the Galapagos, my introduction to connectivity took place right before my eyes. The most fascinating, and I think most important, thing I have ever done was lead a project that interfaced academic knowledge as it cascaded online from 1997 until the summer of 2000. I describe this in detail in chapter 6. I now know from hindsight that what I saw and handled was a playing out of the laws of the new science of networks.

My team had the good luck to notice, and the adventure of prodding, altogether new ways that knowledge started connecting when it landed in the digital soup and began nestling into the nonhierarchical and nonrestrictive matrix of the quickly maturing Internet. I shared the experience with people I would like to thank here for their vision and the key roles they played in making our adventure a success. They are now scattered by the vagaries of the Internet economy, which has washed away a lot of empty ideas but slowed the emergence of some of the best innovations. Our group worked together during a sweet spot in time, and it was a privilege to be their teammate and to count them as friends. These people, listed in their order of appearance, noticed the new behavior of what we were collecting and facilitated its development: Brett Jenkins, Kimberly Patterson, Richard Flynn, Nan Halperin, Anthony Reynolds, and Jennifer Cordi. I am also grateful to Greg Chotkowski who has guided me along the emerging edge of mobile connectivity for the past two years. Tom Koerner has encouraged me to write and I am deeply grateful for his confidence.

My primary goal in writing this book has been to enlist you in the cause of connectivity. It is an idea at least as revolutionary as evolution was when Darwin summoned the courage to tell the world that physical creatures' unique features will flow into their progeny—which seemed to many to somehow replace God. Connectivity, too, is enormously threatening. It is also wonderfully hopeful. It is threatening in education because it centers communication in the student, not the teacher or administrator. It is threatening to all varieties of thought police because everyone can know everything. It is hopeful at many levels, which I will introduce in the pages ahead, but most of all because it provides a global commons of human knowledge in which every person on Earth will share. Connectivity awaits neither technology nor the content to be grazed on the commons. It does not even await a top-down movement, organization, or committee. It grows node-by-node from the inside out. Nodes in connectivity are persons and it is they who do the connecting. Can we hear you yet?

Judy Breck
New York City
July 2003

INTRODUCTION

IT'S THE NETS

The world is reeling from change. As the new century got under way, two big surges (a) terrorism and (b) digital technologies and the Internet—crested at once and slammed the world hard with 9/11 and an economic downturn, which was accelerated by the terrorist attacks. A third thing happening at the same time is just now beginning to be noticed: network science was born. Some very smart people figured out the math on why we are all connected by about six degrees of separation. This book is about how the first two major blows, and a lot of other problems, are being better understood and potentially solved by what we are learning from the third one, the nets. The biggest news from the nets is that the degrees of separation among all people will virtually disappear. For many this has already happened. Millions of us are closely connected through the Internet on our desk or in a bag over our shoulder or through a cell phone that goes where we go. In a quickly expanding human web, we are connected to other people at our will and to enterprises where we do business. Through other sorts of networks we are connected to enormous amounts of information.

There remain billions of people who are not part of these networks. They are getting information from somewhere else, if at all, and those of us who are connected cannot hear them yet.

Underlying the teetering of our times is an older, much-discussed, much-lamented global worry: the failure of education. In the long haul, the new network science will have its broadest and deepest impact in this field. From the progressive promises of the early 1900s, to mid-century angry shouts of "Johnny Can't Read,"[1] to the anguish over "Tragic Inequalities"[2] and into our era of diminishing standards and intellectually insular schools across the globe, little has been found to slow down the dumbing down of our planet. Billions cannot read. College kids in good schools are doing the work their grandparents did in high school. Teaching has become a combat occupation.

Network science offers—and will force upon us—a solution much larger than fixing the schools. What has already occurred within digital networks has eliminated the need for the $3 billion U.S. textbook industry, although the education and publishing establishments have not yet let it go. Hardly just a replacement for textbooks, online knowledge in academic subjects is superior to the printed versions in freshness, cognitive sizzle, and contextual richness. All three of these characteristics—as well as the access to them—are the direct result of network functionality. Network science fundamentally condemns our pervasive standards and curricula, and makes us cringe at the anti-socialization of the separation by grade within schools and from family that is a mainstay of our crumbling education practices.

Chapter 6 describes how human knowledge behaves in networks, which are already the main place students do research at the college level and should be for younger students. Chapter 7 is a network critique of education as we have known it in recent decades. The subjects of the earlier chapters are also relevant to education. By putting them ahead in the sequence of the book, I am emphasizing my belief that education should be approached from the larger world. Understanding what is happening there will prepare us to realize we cannot fix education. We are, instead, able to start over and create something much better on the network platform.

There remains one big step to be taken before the new order of tomorrow, projected by network science, becomes our reality: We need to make sure every person on Earth has a mobile handheld device with which he or she can connect interactively with the meshed nets now forming and thickening around the planet—so that he or she shares in the virtual commons of human knowledge and can be heard.

This book is an argument for universal individual connectivity based on new things we are learning from network science. That science has convinced me, and I think it will convince you, that connecting everyone is a quicker, deeper, and more permanent way to wipe terror off the planet than anything else available. That is reason enough to push up the connecting process. I am equally convinced that the woes of illiteracy and ignorance will dissipate in a fully connected world because the connections into the meshed nets include linkages to a vast virtual storehouse of the common knowledge of humankind. There are many other benefits, and I am sure you will think of ones I have not included, to having the whole human web plugged interactively into our common digital future—for each person to connect and be able to respond. Doing so will virtually erase the degrees of separation across which develop ignorance, misunderstanding, tyrannical control, and, more recently, the digital divide.

The grand vision of interactively connecting us all can no longer be dismissed as an optimist's folly. It is under way and it works, as this vignette from a *New York Times* report describes:

> MANCHESTER, England, May 29, 2003—Three years ago, Shirley Hughes lived a life of dreary routine, collecting welfare checks, bringing up two children as a single mother, passing her evenings in front of the television. Today, she teaches her neighbors how to use computers at a local college while studying for a teaching certificate. At home, she skips *Buffy the Vampire Slayer* in favor of the Internet, which she surfs avidly, downloading patterns for patchwork quilts, her favorite hobby. Ms. Hughes's computer is connected to the Internet "24/7," as she puts it, through a technology known as WI-FI. For her, it has been a virtual passport out of the decaying industrial landscape of East Manchester, a place only now recovering from the end of history's last great commercial revolution.[3]

That passport will transform the future no less than was done by the inventions of the wheel, printing press, and air travel. The more quickly we can get the passport into the hands of all individuals, the sooner our world will calm down and find its way to a golden age of peace and prosperity based on the natural relationships offered by networks.

Hooking everybody in the world up is not at all far-fetched. It is already happening fast. Our option is whether to push to make it happen faster. I hope we do and urge you to help, at the least with your understanding and approval. Our planet now has the technological capability to connect everyone by just one degree of separation. Already, wherever you are, if you have a cell phone, you are one degree separated from me and every other cell phone user anywhere. It is of course true that two people talking over land telephone lines are separated by only one degree, unless they used an operator to connect their call. But their connection is not mobile, limiting both people to holding a wired receiver to their ears, while a cell phone would keep them connected as they move around. Cell phone connections are also different from land lines because their conversations are carried dynamically through meshed nets, with pieces of conversations scattered as they travel and reunited at the receiving end.

What I refer to in this book as *meshed nets* are much more than lines connecting things. They encompass wires of metal and glass, beams of several types for the short distances to your microwave controls and digital highway toll-taker and the long ones of the satellite transmissions that shrink global distances to nanoseconds. As further parts of the meshed nets, all of these are connected to each other and to a lot more: the Internet, every computer and chip attached to the nets from anywhere and, if you will, the network of thoughts in the minds of everyone communicating through the macro meshed nets that now encompass our globe and thicken with every passing day. We are moving rapidly to the day when essentially all digital resources will be located in the meshed nets instead of in a computer a person considers personal, stored on CDs like music used to be, or archived on floppies and tape as we did it in the dim past of a couple of years ago.

The vast majority of websites are already digital files in remote server farms and not on the physical location of the webmaster or domain owner. Web pages are increasingly dynamic, pulling content into their interfaces from distant archives at the command of the human visitor—in effect connecting a fact or thought from a remote location with the current idea in the living visitor's mind. The connections of the telephone industry, the controllers that operate your garage door and home appliances, the cash register where you shop and the transaction you make with your credit card—and a whole lot of other things—are moving very fast to reside and occur within the meshed nets where they can interact dynamically with you and with each other. The device that you will use to interact with all of what is moving into the nets will be a mobile controller with a screen and other interfaces for human connectivity and interaction. It will be a merger and morphing of your laptop, cell phone, credit card, and remote controllers.

It is patently obvious that only those persons who are connected can use the communication, actions, and resources located within the meshed nets. Mobile, handheld access devices are roaring down the pipe to make it not only possible but practical for every person on Earth to have a mobile controller and be connected. That connection will soon become how an individual gets news broadcasts and entertainment media, makes telephone calls, shops, makes purchases and pays for them, pays parking fees and bridge tolls, votes in an election, and gets an education. It is also patently obvious that all of this basic functionality would not be moving onto the Internet and the mobile handheld controllers would not be roaring down the pipe if what I have been describing were some sort of science fiction. This is not a book predicting what the future will be. It is a celebration of what we are learning from the new network science that explains a great deal about what the connecting now under way will mean for humankind. I hope it will convince you to join in executing the action plan suggested in the last chapter to speed the interactive connection of all persons on the planet into the meshed nets.

The new science of networks was born in the academic world, not among the meshed net industries of communication, wiring, hardware, and website authoring. Most of the thought and work on the theories has been in mathematics and the sciences, but it seems very likely that since the changes I have been describing are all about networks, the new science should have some interesting things to say about the new digital connectivity. Indeed it does. In the chapters ahead, I have approached the developing theories of the new network science through topics, now immersed in real-world connectivity as it relates to terror, business, artistic expression, academic knowledge, and education.

Like all the venues where networks are inherent, the venues explored in the chapters are environments of complexity and chaos. As Edward Lorenz pointed out four decades ago, at nearly the same time sociologist Stanley Milgram discovered we are all connected by about six degrees:

"One flap of a seagull's wings would be enough to alter the course of the weather forever."[4] His idea, which came to be known as the butterfly effect, is the "essence of chaos," in the words of the Cal Tech physics department.[5] An aspect of the chaos that has been dominoing around the globe is located within the Muslim world, which is now reeling with big changes as everyone else watches them anxiously. Muslims are dealing with the reality that democracy may actually diminish centuries-old authority wielded by clerics, warlords, thugs, and wealth. It is not at all clear what is going to happen—whether the democracy can and will take hold. The new global meshed nets will play an increasing role as tribes and cultures long controlled from the top down will be transformed into something very different when they are populated by individuals—all of whom have handheld interactive connections into global networks of communication and knowledge—who can hear and be heard. Network theory will argue in these pages that the order that will emerge from that sort of chaos will work to everyone's benefit. The order arising from the chaos of democracy will be in stark contrast to the destructive chaos that bubbles beneath the order now imposed by the powerful.

It is astoundingly good luck that the new network ideas have so suddenly appeared, just now when they can helpfully shed light into the human networking revolution brought about by digital technologies that led to the rise of the Internet. Ten years ago if you were to ask cosmologists, mathematicians, physicists, biologists, sociologists, or historians to name the core structure of their fields it is unlikely any of them—and certainly not all—would have replied: It's the nets. But that is the categorical assertion being made these days by first one discipline and then another and another. A seminal textbook on network evolution, published in 2003 by Oxford University Press, prefaces its chapters with these statements: "Only recently have we realized that we reside in a world of networks. . . . 'Network' turns out to be a central notion in time. . . ."[6]

In the pages ahead we will touch on networks pointed to by the experts in diverse disciplines. There is another network notion, however, that is central to this book. I submit that you and I, and as soon as possible every person on Earth, have a stunning new facility to use networks dynamically as a tool of communication, community, enterprise, expression, and learning. I call this activity using *dynamic nets*, which we are already doing in a limited way with our desktop computers, laptops, and cell phones. But we have barely begun, and how quickly we empower everyone on the planet to use dynamic nets is up to us.

As indicated above, the almost sudden realization that the platforms of so many aspects of reality are formed by web-structured networks has its origins in the study over the past couple of decades of chaos and complexity. A fascinating question at the core of these subjects is how order, instead of entropy, spontaneously occurs within complexity. There is a large, growing, wonderful body of literature on that subject; the sources among these that I have used are listed in my endnotes. I make no claim to be a complexity authority but have thought a lot about another nonlinear field. I have studied painting and aesthetics where ideas surprisingly similar to network theories are used to ponder the complexity of artifacts from which beauty and meaning can arise.

From a different angle, I offer a generalist network perspective acquired during several years of intense hands-on experience in making and linking up content on the Internet. The staff I assembled to do the linking work included PhD's and PhD and master's degree candidates specializing in the major academic fields. They are very bright people with whom I was able to speculate from the inside about the formation of the Internet, as the formation was going on and we, in fact, helped to build it. This book uses a macro view that grew out of that experience—of the startling and empowering networking not within but *among* major aspects of all of the fields mentioned above, and others. Because they are all set free from hierarchy and represented digitally, the fields can be and are effortlessly linked within the Internet, and from there interfaced into the human web of connected people with rapidly increasing effectiveness by mobile and handheld devices. From the webbed relations in one grand soup of communication, ideas, and human activities emerge many newly understood network phenomena. And, as we will see, the individual person emerges as well, with the power to cast interactive dynamic nets.

If you now have Internet access or a cell phone, you are already sending your own dynamic nets of activity through that thickening mix of action and ideas that are the meshed nets. Increasingly using dynamic nets within the interconnected networks is what you and everyone else will do to accomplish increasingly more activities. I demonstrate in the pages ahead why I am convinced that the global goals of peace, freedom, security, health, prosperity, literacy, and learning will be advanced importantly by equipping every individual on the planet with a handheld device that gives its owner the facility to use dynamic nets. (If you are saying to yourself, don't let the bad guys have them, you need to realize the bad guys already do.)

NOTES

1. Rudolf Flesch, *Why Johnny Can't Read* (New York: Harper and Row, 1955).

2. Jonathan Kozol, *Savage Inequalities: Children in American Schools* (New York, Crown, 1991).

3. Mark Landler, "With Wireless, an English City Reaches across Digital Divide," *New York Times Online*, www.nytimes.com/2003/05/31/technology/31WIFI.html [accessed 31 May 2003].

4. California Institute of Technology: Condensed Matter Physics, "The Butterfly Effect," www.cmp.caltech.edu/~mcc/chaos_new/Lorenz.html [accessed 31 May 2003].

5. Landler, "With Wireless."

6. S. N. Dorogovtsev and J. F. F. Mendes, *Evolution of Networks: From Biological Nets to the Internet and WWW* (Oxford: Oxford University Press, 2003).

1

DYNAMIC NETS: YOUR PERSONAL CONTROLLER

> All had then been lost and no help for it, for they would have been penned up in Ilius like sheep, had not the sire of gods and men been quick to mark, and hurled a fiery flaming thunderbolt which fell just in front of Diomed's horses with a flare of burning brimstone. The horses were frightened and tried to back beneath the car, while the reins dropped from Nestor's hands. Then he was afraid and said to Diomed, "Son of Tydeus, turn your horses in flight; see you not that the hand of Jove is against you?[1]
>
> —Homer

Jove often cast lighting into human affairs to make something happen. What if you could do that too? If you have a handheld digital device you can do just what Jove did, although you scatter very few electrons. With increasing elegance and range, you are able to cast dynamic nets to communicate and change things—to hear and be heard. A dynamic net is what you use to participate in the network milieu. It is your individual way of entering and using the networks, linking and interacting with the nodes you need for a particular task.

A sample from the real world is the best way to show you what this participation is and to give you a look at a network as tool a person uses to achieve something. As this example illustrates, thinking of what is happening as a single dynamic net gives you a simple way to conceptualize a very complicated situation and provides you with a means to relate all of its parts in a coherent pattern. Here is a dynamic net activated by a birder among whooper swan enthusiasts:

> Say you're slogging through a bog in northern Finland when you come across a Whooper Swan building its nest. By pushing a few numbers on your GPS phone, the exact position of your sighting, along with species, gender and time of day, is sent to a worldwide group of registered users who have indicated their interest in Finland's national bird. Instantly, nature enthusiasts around the globe are brought together by your discovery and can share not just your excitement but your data as well.[2]

This description is from a March 2003 Hewlett Packard advertisement. The GPS phone is the birder's cell phone, which he is using to activate a dynamic net to engage and exchange species locations in real time. He is sharing his excitement at his sighting and simultaneously enriching a central datanet that stores knowledge useful to scientists and birders in protecting birds and their habitats. The birder sighting the swan simultaneously employs the dynamic net to inform a global swarm of swan aficionados.

Many nets within the macro net environment are part of the dynamic net initiated by the whooper swan sighting. The GPS software within the birder's cell phone captures signals from at least four global positioning satellites (GPS) to determine their positions at the time the birder saw the swan so the phone can calculate its own exact location from the data it has received. That location is incorporated into the birder's message announcing the sighting. The cell phone then links into the global communication network, scattering parts of the birder's message as packets, bouncing about through the nets gathered around the planet, seeking to find and enter the bird information datanet whose address is encoded in the birder's message. When all the packets are reassembled at the bird information datanet, they are directed into its internal mininet devoted to whooper swans. From there, the mininet is enriched by the new data, which it passes along internally to related mininets such as the sections for nest building and birds of Finland. The arrival of new data triggers a search within the birds datanet for people who want information on the swans and assembles a list of those it identifies. The output center then sends a message noting the time and location of the swan sighting to each person on the list, once again scattering packets across the global communication network. The receiving local nets (in desktops, laptops, or cell phones) process the message, store it for interfacing and tell their humans with a visual posting or beep that the message has arrived. When the humans open the interface and look at the sighting data other sets of networks are activated in those persons' senses and minds. Any of the receiving humans could then be triggered to output a secondary message to notify other datanets and/or people of the new swan sighting, thereby starting the activation of other dynamic nets. The birder used a dynamic net to distribute word of his sighting. That dynamic net emerged from the enormous macro complexity of interactive networks, drawing on whatever connections and resources were useful. The dynamic net ceased to exist when it had served its purpose.

We have been looking at an entirely new sort of interconnection among people, ideas, and media that began to emerge quite recently from the multiplying complexity of our networked world, which will soon be essential to almost everything we do. The interconnections, like flashes of lightning across a summer sky, are temporary events. As the complexity of intermeshed networks on our planet multiplies, the number and kinds of interconnections—and our control over them—increase; they are rapidly becoming the main way that we do many, many things. The concept explained in the following paragraph by Notre Dame professor of physics Albert-László Barabási crystallized for me what I had seen flashing across Internet content, digital expressive media, and cell phone social swarms. I realized the events were all one sort of thing, which I came to think of as *dynamic nets*. Their definition is a lot like the definition of a gestalt: the whole is more than the sum of the parts. But here the whole is ephemeral because it only exists while a set of parts are functioning together. As Barabási says, here referring to genes, the whole is dynamic:

> Not too long ago it was widely believed that everything that matters for any organism's biological history is encoded in the genes. Post genomic biology, though still in its infancy, is already fighting an important battle. It aims to diminish the all-encompassing role historically attributed to individual genes. Genes are known to play a *structural* role, determining the scope and make of proteins and passing this information in a hereditary manner to subsequent generations. Recently, however, scientists have discovered that genes also play an important *functional* role as mem-

> bers of a complex cellular network. This functional role is apparent only in the dynamic context in which an individual gene interacts with many other cellular components.[3]

When it becomes dynamic, the cellular network does tasks different from its structural duties that are accomplished by its static and inert structure. That is, of course, true of the mechanical world. Your car is just a conglomeration of metal, rubber, upholstery, and gasoline as it sits in your garage, and something more when you are cruising down the interstate and the conglomeration is functioning dynamically. Concepts explored in this book give us insight into what kinds of things happen when networks function. In the car analogy, your car is performing in its simplest and least meaningful way when considered alone as a single car moving along a road. Considered more broadly, the car is part of a macro network of activity made up of all the cars in the traffic it is in, the condition of the road, how the weather is affecting traffic, the individual destinations of everyone in the cars and the competence and alertness of every driver on the road. That seems like a description of chaos, or at least of complexity. Yet within everything else that is going on, you back your car out of the garage, drive onto a freeway, exit at a mall, park in the mall lot, move in and out through stores, return with packages to your car, go under the freeway to a gas station and fill your tank, drive by a friend's house to drop off a package, drive home, and pull into your garage. Within all the complex motions of every other car and person, the pattern of your movements served your purposes. A dynamic net does the same for you virtually. What you will be able to do with dynamic nets is getting broader and richer with every passing day.

We will not need to elucidate here the intricacies of the mathematics, biology, sociology, history, and other intellectual fields to appreciate that the functional/dynamic events that arise from entangling networks are exciting new players in human thought and affairs. Better credentialed writers are doing a wonderful job of creating the literature that explains network theories. Still, if we decided to take the time to learn the sciences, we could not do it anyway because nobody has the theories worked out yet. Cornell University's applied mathematics professor Steven Strogatz, who, along with Duncan Watts, developed the original small world theory, explained in his 2003 book *Sync*, that:

> Researchers are only now beginning to unravel the structure of complex networks. . . . Even if we were given the complete wiring diagrams for any of these systems—a list of all the nodes (genes, species, people) and the connections between them—we wouldn't know what to compute. The mass of data would be overwhelming. Until we know what we're looking for, the secrets of complex networks will remain elusive. What we need now are ideas: simple, organizing principles to guide us through the morass of data.[4]

Strogatz goes on to say that history tells us the "most penetrating ideas will come from mathematics,"[5] which is likely to be true for the theories. But, for the time being, a simple convention of calling all temporary sets of connections that support an event by the same name—*dynamic nets*—seems useful as we turn to a practical application side that urgently calls us to action. We can improve our world by speeding up the process of putting dynamic nets into everyone's hands. Dynamic nets empower the individual socially and intellectually, and pull the teeth of tyrants: Like Jove armed with his quiver of thunderbolts, men, women and children equipped with a handheld interactive device are empowered to cast dynamic nets that engage them in radically new ways to communicate, express ideas, do business, and learn. The intricacies of education theory will be forced by the great hook-up into the meshed nets to be examined by network science. The traditional world of an isolated group of learners under the control of a single pedagogue is disappearing and should be eliminated more quickly. A new pedagogy is needed, and rightfully should be developed along with our understanding of the transforming aspects of the nets in other fields.

But our main focus in this book is the practical side, which is compelling! It is a sufficient call to action to learn that dynamic nets in the hands of enough people will confound the breeding grounds for terrorism by liberating connections among individuals and information, which is the subject of chapter 3. The four chapters after that describe how dynamic nets can and inexorably will cause other sweeping changes, serving as a mobile platform for how we do business, giving birth to new expressive media, transforming how what we know is archived and mirrored to the mind, and providing the priesthoods of established education with a long overdue run for their money—in a pursuit they seem likely to lose. The areas of impact I have chosen for major chapters of this book are certainly not the only ones that lie ahead. They are the ones where I have had the most experience; I hope you will apply explanations of dynamic nets to your own areas of interest and expertise to discover if the principles discussed generally are valid there. After reading the first two chapters, you should have no difficulty jumping to any of the remaining chapters in whatever order fits your interests.

Do not discount your potential for helping. The networked world is not being formed by anyone in particular, nor is it being put together or controlled from the top. Always, dynamic nets grow by spreading outward, existing virtually. Tim Berners-Lee, inventor of the World Wide Web, explains a deceptive simplicity:

> What was often difficult for people to understand about the design was that there was nothing else beyond URLs, http, and HTML. There was no central computer "controlling" the Web, no single network on which these protocols worked, not even an organization anywhere that "ran" the Web. The Web was not a physical "thing" that existed in a certain "place," It was a "space" in which information could exist.[6]

The content of the Web and the entire Internet is created one page at a time and grows outward into weblets and clusters; there is no way to grow it or control it from the top because it will support no hierarchy beyond nesting a few pages here and there. WI-FI spreads its coverage like a lily pad over a pond, just as wired access spreads by radiating from Internet service providers one hook-up at a time. Least of all could dynamic nets be built from the top down because dynamic nets hook themselves together emerging at our personal will. Like the Web, they arise from the linking made possible by increasing the number of persons using digital communication networks and by making their access mobile. The more these factors increase, the more people everywhere will benefit from dynamic nets.

I have a suggested plan of action to speed things up. It is described in more detail in the eighth and concluding chapter. These are the main elements of that plan:

Beam, upgrade, standardize, and spread broadband wireless access until it is available everywhere on the planet.

- Complete and distribute to everyone on Earth a cheap, mobile, handheld, interactive device (which is called simply a *handheld* in this book). The handheld becomes a person's telephone, pager, text message tool, information organizer, checkbook, and Internet browser.
- On every handheld, include interfaces for acquiring literacy and useful knowledge online.
- Enhance the knowledge assets for dynamic nets.
- Unwire the schools and transform the school technology coordinator into the school network coordinator.

Each element in this plan is already developing spontaneously, and the dynamic nets we currently use are the product of the synergy of these elements. Dynamic nets are already here and are a way to define the common denominator of human participation in the digital milieu. Dynamic nets constitute the next big thing and their appearance is recent—almost sudden. The digital age has taken shape with an ongoing rollout of big things making massive changes: desktop computers, the Internet and the World Wide Web, wiring, unwiring, and cell phones. Over time, those and other factors have formed an environment that has recently done a phase transition like water into steam—passing the tipping point to create the new era of dynamic nets. The tipping set off a cascade of dynamic interactivity within the amalgam of things digital. Old networks and nets from suites of entirely new networks increasingly meshed into the rapidly expanding macro dynamic net environment where many of the basic elements of human affairs now take place. A human event that transpires in the new environment occurs within a temporary and unique spate of connections that form a dynamic net for that event. The event is neither technology nor the digital content that swirls through the net; it is the function of the dynamic connections that form a brief particular network—like a burst of lightning. A dynamic net is a unique enabling pattern that ceases to exist when the event ends.

My use of the term *dynamic* for nets has a precedent in the standard term *dynamic page* in website parlance. A static Web page is the page generated by the html that supports the page. Whenever a static page is viewed on a Web browser, it is always the same; to change the page you must change the html that defines it. A dynamic page is put together on the fly, combining instructions it receives from its html, the person opening it, and distant sources for what it displays. The dynamic page uses static parts in combination with parts from elsewhere to assemble itself for the immediate purpose of the user who then views and acts upon the configuration the dynamic page displays.

The dynamic nets discussed in this book are structured in a similar way by instructions housed in static networks that are activated, interacted with, and participated in mentally by the users of the dynamic nets they create. News of the sighting of the swan traveled through a dynamic net activated by the birder through the enormous complexity of meshed nets, drawing upon whatever pathways and resources were useful. The dynamic net ceased to exist when all the interested parties got the news. The dynamic net is an extension and tool of the person who casts it, giving you and me a way to control and get things done within the increasingly pervasive network arena.

The structure of dynamic nets is weblike, giving the nets a versatility much greater than linear connectors. Dynamic nets are nonlinear connections of lines among nodes of communication, but they can reach into all sorts of archival, cognitive, economic, and social networks as well. Did you notice that what the birder was thinking and communicating was part of the dynamic nets he was using? In part, the shapes of the nets were the shapes of his thoughts. That is not, of course, true of the pattern the packets found through the communication hookups, but the pattern among the birders reflected to some degree their shared interest in whooper swans.

As chapter 3 discusses, sociologists are taking a hard look at people swarms caused by cell phones among teenagers, political activists, and others. In infinitely more complex patterning, the networks of neurons and ideas in the minds of the humans using their dynamic nets are functionally part of the nets. By our definition of them, *dynamic nets* also do a good job of defining what we use in our heads when we think. Dr. Peter J. Bentley of University College London takes a peek at some awesome complexity where a dynamic flicker of electrical and chemical interconnections is the physical basis of a thought:

> You have around 100 billion neurons inside your head. If you can imagine that each is connected to an average of 10,000 of its companions, you

> might begin to realize just how complicated your brain is. So although a single neuron is capable of quite simple computations, when you have enough of them and when you connect enough of them together, you result in sufficient complexity for mysterious things like learning, memory, and even consciousness to emerge. It is the network of neurons that enables us to think.[7]

The complex brain experiences higher thought—a provocative hint that the more complex our meshing of the Internet, communications network and other nets, the more complex will become the dynamic nets we can enjoy. Chapter 5 will explore this last point in some depth, highlighting that virtual digital nets are the most efficacious and elegant mirrors of thought we have yet experienced.

Dynamic nets in the digital arena are new because the massive networked digital milieu is new. These new dynamic nets are contributing significantly to defining the future. They already reach deeply into global communication and commerce. They have been used to connect al Qaeda cells and by the armed coalition that swarmed across Iraq in the spring of 2003. The generation who are now teenagers and children use cell phones to generate dynamic nets in ways that mystify their elders. A dynamic net is not just access to information and other people. The power and impact of nets are more than the sum of the parts—gestalts. Dynamic nets are purposeful gestalts, not just surfing. They organize pertinent patterns of nodes giving us some control in the complexity of the Internet, mobile phone connectivity and other networks in which we are increasingly moving around.

Until we understand that underlying the structure of the future is the dynamism of networking, we stand arms folded staring into the past. We do not have an information highway because a highway goes just one place at a time. We do have a cognitive network that is reflecting what we know and doing so with an eloquence that has barely budded so far. That virtual cognitive network is meshed with other networks that are massively interconnecting our transactions and reducing the approximately six degrees of separation of every person on the planet to less than the time it takes to enter ten thumb clicks. The equality and individuality of each of us will be determined by our control over dynamic nets. We will make our planet a far better place by putting the ability to cast dynamic nets into every person's hands.

The changeover will be complete when the link of every individual is personal and mobile into dynamic nets he or she uses in communication and information networks. How soon that personal ownership of participation will be depends on what we do about it. Dynamic nets are already here and are taking over major aspects of human affairs and thought. We use them from the still-primitive wireless handheld, from wired or wireless laptops, and from stationary wired desktop or mainframe computer links. From any of those devices a person can be a participant in a dynamic net. As I write, the desktop experience for the human is far superior most of the time to most handheld interfacing processes. The desktop will fade like a rotary phone when broadband increases, content accommodates, and the mobile handhelds merge with the laptops and cell phones into the handheld of the future. Most pundits these days are predicting this will happen by 2006.

What will be the standard device of the future? For the purposes of this book, that device will be small and portable, and will contain the following:

- full telephone service
- access to streaming video and audio of all television channels and radio frequencies
- broadband Internet connection and interface
- a full desktop suite of word processing, spreadsheet, and document management software
- the capacity to download from the Internet as needed everything else the person who owns it needs and uses as his or her personal computer
- credit input/output (replacing credit cards)
- driver's license, passport, and other confidential documents
- electronic house, office, and car keys and remote control for unlimited devices from the garage door to a safe deposit box

Does this seem like a staggering amount of content? True, but soon the content will almost all be in cyberspace and the device will become nothing much more than a controller. Within a very few years handhelds—and desktop computers—will contain very little internal software and few files. When a program or file is needed, it will be temporarily downloaded from the Internet or it will be run on a remote server somewhere and controlled from the handheld. Similarly, the handheld owner's data will be stored on a remote server. Thus the handheld will become increasingly less memory-intensive, lighter, cheaper, and less of a problem if it is lost. School children will have a single handheld instead of books, paper, and backpacks. If they lose or break their handheld it will be no more serious than losing or breaking the TV remote controller is now. The standard device of the future will, in fact, be the individual's controller for dynamic nets.

It is a mistake to assume that tomorrow's cheap and easy control of the dynamic nets means the handheld device we will use to relate to them will not be sophisticated and elegant. Quite opposite will be true. We are still using the interface tools created twenty-five years ago that have acquired the nickname WIMP: Windows, Icons, Menus, and Pointer. My guess is the common handheld of the future will be something along the following lines: The standard two-dimensional display will appear on a thin, flexible film. (Eventually, holographs will arise from the film for three-dimensional displays.) The film will be available in sizes ranging from a few inches, so you can roll it up and stick it in your pocket, to whatever wall size fits conveniently above your work table, to something big enough for a billboard.

Very small displays will project on the inner surfaces of goggles and inside of scientific and surgical instruments. It will not be out of the question to cover a football field for a half-time show with a film sheet interface of a Web page. A smart cylinder with the dimensions of a fat pencil will attach to the film to receive the Internet (including all phone, financial, and other communication, by now all embedded in the Internet) and feed into the interface film. The smart cylinders will have ports for using nonfilm monitors, a keyboard—which can optionally consist of a keyboard image on the film interface, a headset for music and phone calls, and other attachments we have not thought of yet.

The tipping point has not yet been reached—but we will tip away from the desktop in a spectacular phase transition about, I would guess, 2005. When the tipping occurs, it will be obvious that the practice of wiring computers to desks in offices, homes, and school has ended and the standard computer will accompany each person constantly like today's wristwatch and pocket money do. The first issue of *UNWIRED* (from the publishers of *WIRED*) came out in May 2003. This peek into the future appears on the *fast forward* page, showing a mocked up wireless service bill dated April 2006 that includes these charges for which a handheld had been used: key retrieval, music download, traffic zone fee, toll, video download, e-book download of book chapters, film download, parking fee, vending machine "6 oz Red Bull AM," game download, in-flight WI-FI, salted peanuts.[8]

All these features are in the pipe and on the way. At some point in the near future there will be no device-related reason to argue that everyone on Earth cannot have an individual handheld with remote access—equipping all to use dynamic nets. A dark side is exposed by those who question that everyone should be included in having personal mobile access. It seems self-evident that the more social and economic essentials that are embedded into the Internet, the more crucial it becomes for all individuals to link to the digital arena. The handheld is rapidly becoming the cheapest and most efficient way to establish a link for each person into the network environment, where events are taking place that affect a substantial amount of everyone's daily life and ability to pursue their happiness. The dynamic participation by everyone is appropriate and, as we will explore, a key to the success of the human race. This question on the dark side rests on whether powerful people are prepared to relinquish political and cultural control to all (any?) individuals. My answer to that is they will have no choice, as I explain in chapter 3.

If you are not of a technical bent, and do not really care how dynamic nets work, you may be thinking ahead to the amazing potential we are already glimpsing for how they are changing, and I believe bettering, our world. You may be imagining a young teenager in remote Mongolia tapping about in the MIT Civil and Engineering tutorials[9] (which are online and free as I write this). Or you might see a young wife sitting in the back of her husband's store in Morocco watching a Paris television newscast on her handheld, which is tucked out of public view under her traditional head covering. As she watches a news feature on spring fashions, she is chatting through the handheld's headset with her older sister in Cairo. High on my list of instances-to-come is a ten-year-old sitting cross-legged on his bed in an East St. Louis housing project using his handheld to take the standardized online test for plane geometry, which will be his last certification needed to exempt him from public school so he can go into the Mississippi River Valley hydraulic engineering apprenticeship project. You may be pondering what it will take for these individuals to have the handhelds and to know how to use them. I think a better question is whether there could possibly be anything to prevent it.

Handheld Internet access should cost less than $200 by 2005 and the price will plummet after that. When it is nothing more than a film and controller the size of a pen, it will become free because advertisers will place images on the handhelds and absorb the cost to the user. Fantastic? No, inevitable. The economic impact is not going to be in creating the handhelds but in absorbing the demise of the industries that are now supported by all the things from telephones to textbooks that the handhelds will virtually replace.

The general way in which the symphony of things work within and among the handhelds can be conceptualized as the implementation and use of dynamic nets. In the next chapter we will see that what happens in a network is the same whether it is linking ideas, images, bird nesting information, a conversation, or an idea in someone's head. The environment is a network that has the structure of a web; when it is used, portions of one or more networks are activated into a dynamic net. When a kid in Tikrit is thinking about petroleum chemistry while working on an online tutorial from Rome, while linked via a virtual white board to a tutor in Toledo, and forwarding an invitation to a chemistry newsgroup of a demonstration the next week at an oil refinery near Mosul, everything that is happening is a part of a dynamic net. The kid's thoughts, the links among the tutorial pages, the routes taken by the text messages, the patterns of communication among members of the newsgroup and their swarm the next week to the demonstration interact within dynamic nets.

One question is likely to be holding up your enthusiasm. All of what I have been describing would be out of the reach of the Earth's billion or so illiterate people and many more who are only semiliterate. Before moving ahead, we need to look at what networks and handhelds will mean for literacy. We begin in the deepest jungle.

LEARNING TO READ

The ten-year-old turning the pages of a picture alphabet book had no knowledge that the twentieth century had just arrived. A few minutes earlier he had found his way into the cabin where he had been born. He had paid little attention to the skeletons of his biological father and mother, and of the tiny baby ape whose body Kala, the only mother he knew, had left in the cradle when she removed the infant human as a substitute for her own dead baby. The boy had seen many carcasses in the jungle where he lived, but he had never seen another human being, or anything that was a picture like those he discovered in the book he had just found. Edgar Rice Burroughs describes the scene:

> The pictures caught his fancy most, though the strange little bugs which covered the pages where there were no pictures excited his wonder and deepest thought. Squatting upon his haunches on the table top in the cabin his father had built—his smooth, brown, naked little body bent over the book which rested in his strong, slender hands, and his great shock of long, black hair falling about his well shaped head and bright, intelligent eyes—Tarzan of the apes, little primitive man, presented a picture filled, at once, with pathos and with promise—an allegorical figure of the primordial groping through the black night of ignorance toward the light of learning.[10]

As Tarzan began opening the books that filled chests his parents had brought from England, he did not know what a book was but he could understand some of the pictures. He saw images of a monkey, an elephant, a snake, and other animals he knew well. There were other recognizable shapes, the most interesting of which were creatures that looked like him, the misfit white ape of his home troop. In the chapter titled "The Light of Knowledge," Burroughs describes how Tarzan persisted through his teen years to decipher the mysterious little bugs and to learn to read.

Throughout the twentieth century, legions of children groped through the black night of ignorance to no avail. Tarzan, with no human help, used a couple of chests full of books to find his way into the light of learning. Imagine, if you will, what it will mean to the ten-year-olds of the twenty-first century when they all have handhelds. Here is a description of one sample from the current state-of-the-art of personal computer devices for children:

> Toy and parenting organizations honored Zip the Robot with five different awards for excellence and educational value! Zip the Robot is loved by both boys and girls and is a fun-tabulous way to introduce younger children to computing. Colorful, talking "notebook" boasts over 50 enjoyable and educational multimedia activities to boost your child's skills in math, vocabulary, grammar, logic, and memory. Mouse and mouse pad included. When your child has mastered the existing games, you can expand Zip's value with our Oregon Scientific Smart Cards (sold separately). For ages 5 and up.[11]

Zip the Robot, which costs about $50, is a small, colorful laptop that does not connect to the Internet. Its software cards have digital exercises for the subjects listed above. Because the exercises are digital, they could be, and probably are at least in similar form, easily placed on the Internet. There is already a bountiful supply of primers, dictionaries, exercises, and reading material overflowing the Internet, including a great deal in just about every language, from Abadani to Zarma,[12] spoken or read by anyone anywhere.

I am often challenged when I express my optimism for learning from the Internet by the perceived prohibition the necessity for literacy would be to universal access. Maybe it is the other way around. I think so. Perhaps it was a stretch, even though it makes a good story, for Edgar Rice Burroughs to describe how Tarzan learned to read by himself by deciphering the "little bugs" he discovered in books. It is a lot easier to imagine a young kid in a Brazilian jungle village using her handheld to explore websites that explain reading and sound out words that accompany digital images. And such a child would surely have at least some human help, not finding herself totally alone, as Tarzan was, in the black night of ignorance. We will explore the role of handhelds in diminishing ignorance in chapters 3 and 7. My conviction is that there is no huge learning curve that will keep any of us from using dynamic nets and that the nets themselves are very good teachers of reading.

What my collision with network theory has jolted me into realizing is that we have not yet comprehended the unifying and driving force that will forever alter the allegory invented by Edgar Rice Burroughs. It is not so crucial that the jungle is gone, that the apocryphal apes threaten no more, that the global positioning system tells all wanderers exactly where they are. The allegory has lost its pathos and fulfills its promise because the primordial grouping through the black night of ignorance is ending in the digital dawn. Three traditional steps are still required to cross the threshold to full participation in the connectedness of the meshed nets. One must know the 3Rs to be competent at using dynamic nets. The problem comes with a built-in solution. As people obtain their own handhelds they will learn the 3Rs. The population of the world will genuinely become equalized away from ignorance. A person with a handheld, of any age and culture, will have a very good chance to learn to read on her own. The handhelds will certainly be far more effective than minimal literacy programs. They can do a better job of teaching reading than semiliterate teachers. Handhelds also have a self-contained library, used in common by everyone on Earth and giving every reader virtually unlimited material to consume—in contrast to so many places around the world now where even the skilled literate have a paucity of quality reading material.

Perhaps literacy into the future means learning to read English. If that is true, the handhelds import correct English into the farthest regions, provide dictionaries and translators, and contain massive amounts and choices of reading materials. The literature of many sciences and technologies are mainly in English and nearly all of that literature is now on the Internet. There are many languages whose corpus of literature is quite small. The migration of these bodies of literature into digital form and then on to the Internet may in fact preserve them into the future. The grammars and translators for these languages online make them available to anyone who has an interest and prevent them from disappearing if the hardcopies are lost and their speakers diminish.

Where computers dominate learning arenas a two-step process is the frequent approach: first teach young students the 3Rs and, as they get older, guide them to locate things to study on the Internet under the watchful eyes of teachers, curricula standards, and traditional structures of academic subjects. In chapter 7 there is a discussion of the second of these steps.

The first step, the 3Rs, is pretty much the same thing as literacy with arithmetic added. Reading, writing, and arithmetic have long been considered tools of access to further learning and the minimum requirement for anyone to be empowered as a full citizen of society. It may already be true that learning to cast dynamic nets is the necessary and basic tool for learning—it is the key tool for learning everything else, including the 3Rs. A little skill at casting dynamic nets will snag and haul the reading, writing, and arithmetic into your hands. Is there a better, or even any, option for learning the 3Rs if you are in an isolated village or jungle hut with no teacher? Certainly a handheld with reading tutorials would get the literacy job done better than undertaking Tarzan's task of deciphering "little bugs." Once you learn to read on the handheld you would not then be limited, as Tarzan was, to only the books his parents had brought to their hut a decade before; you could read just about anything ever written in any place or time.

Your reaction to this picture may be that your children are going to have personalized phonics instruction by an excellent teacher, your own support and coaching at home, and a terrific library right on the wall of their bedroom. I will not argue against that. It is wonderful, although you might be surprised by how much language skill they are sharpening by texting back and forth with their friends by cell phone. But what about the kids in a south Chicago housing project, and little girls on farms near the Yellow River in China, and young Nigerians who live in remote villages, and older illiterate people everywhere? Any of them, with their own handheld, could have you as their online tutor and encourager—and with their access to the meshed nets they would have far larger libraries than the one on the wall in your children's bedroom. My guess is that software could do nearly as good a job as an excellent human teacher in coaching them in reading. A book that a donkey delivered in 2001 to the Afghan mountain kid we will meet in chapter 3 had animal pictures. With a handheld obtained in 2004 he can cast a dynamic net into a website that offers pictures of the same animals in the book, but in the virtual version there is a button to click to display the printed word for the animal he views in a language of his choice and another button to click to hear the correct pronunciation of that word in the language he picks. To put the ability to use the meshed nets of communication and Internet content dynamically into the hands of people who do not know the 3Rs is to give them a beacon to follow out of the darkness of ignorance. To hold off until they learn the 3Rs before connecting them to the human web does not make sense.

NOTES

1. Homer, *The Iliad*, VIII. trans. Samuel Butler, www.uoregon.edu/~joelja/iliad.html#b8 [accessed 27 April 2003].

2. "Birdlife Finland," www.hp.com/country/us/eng/msg/corp/htmlbirding.html Hewlett Packard, 30 March 2003.

3. Albert-László Barabási, *Linked* (Cambridge, Mass.: Perseus, 2002), 183.

4. Steven Strogatz, *Sync: The Emerging Science of Spontaneous Order* (New York: Hyperion, 2003), 231.

5. Steven Strogatz, *Sync.*

6. Tim Berners-Lee, *Weaving the Web* (San Francisco: Harper, 1999), 36.

7. Peter J. Bentley, *Digital Biology* (New York: Simon & Schuster, 2001), 72.

8. *UNWIRED.* Condé Nast Publications, May 2003, 60.

9. MIT OpenCourseWare, ocw.mit.edu/global/department1.html [accessed 5 May 2003].

10. Edgar Rice Burroughs, *Tarzan of the Apes* (New York: Penguin Books, 1990), 53.

11. Oregon Scientific ZIP the Robot Learning PC, www.dynadirect.com/gs-14894.html [accessed 25 April 2003].

12. "Language Dictionaries and Translators," www.word2word.com/dictionary.html [accessed 25 April 2003].

2

HOW NETS WORK: THE NEW SCIENCE OF NETWORKS

> In the twentieth century we went as far as we could to uncover and describe the components of complex systems. Our quest to understand nature has hit a glass ceiling because we do not yet know how to fit the pieces together. The complex issues with which we are faced, in fields from communication systems to cell biology, demand a brand-new framework. Embarking on the journey ahead without a map would be hopeless. Fortunately the ongoing network revolution has already provided many of the key maps.
>
> —Albert-László Barabási[1]

The insight that sparked this book is very simple. It flashed through my mind in March 2003 as I rode on a train returning from Washington to New York City. I was astounded! Quite suddenly I realized that one simple idea lurked deep within each of the entire spectrum of things I had been thinking about for a very long time. The call I felt in high school to political ideas led me into campaign activities and a degree in political science. In the 1960s, as an advertising copywriter, my focus was on media communication: how to convey ideas in print and over the air on radio and television. For the better part of the 1970s and 1980s my main avocation was learning about painting and aesthetics. From Rudolf Arnheim's writing I came to understand a painting as a gestalt, where the meaning radiates from a whole that is more than the sum of the parts. More than twenty years ago I began my love affair with desktop publishing and for the last ten years the Internet has been my occupation and preoccupation. Very recently a client of mine who is a visionary in the cell phone content field opened to me an exciting new vista of ideas. During all these years I have been active in education, from teaching high school when I was 23, through program, project, and volunteer activities, clear up to the seventh-grade weekly class I taught in the 2002–03 school year. Watching the still-brown fields of late winter pass by the window, I realized that the fundamental operating principle for every one of my favorite subjects, and of many more, is the nets.

Since my epiphany on the train, I have read and learned a lot about networks, and the initial insight has held up. There is a great deal of fascinating material to explore on the subject. I recommend it to you and refer to some of it now and then throughout this book. You will find formative ideas and can become an observer to a science aborning! Three leading explorers of the new network science each published a book in the past year. I learned about the nets mainly from their writing, which is cited in the endnotes. Steven Strogatz, whose book *SYNC*[2] relates the new network story and much more, held faculty positions at Harvard and MIT before coming to Cornell in 1994 where he is a professor of applied mathematics. Duncan J. Watts was Strogatz's student when they teamed up in the work that led to the discovery of small-world networks. Watts is now associate professor of sociology at Columbia. His 2003 book *Six Degrees*[3] is primer on networks and includes an extensive bibliography. Albert-László Barabási is a professor of physics at Notre Dame, where he led the team that discovered the scale-free aspect of small-world networks. Barabási's book *Linked*[4] completes the trilogy that substantially contributed to my understanding and is often quoted in these pages.

In *Six Degrees*, Watts described the state of the new network science in 2003:

> In the world of networks, sociologists, economists, mathematicians, computer scientists, biologists, engineers, and physicists, all have something to offer each other and much to learn. No one discipline, no single approach, has a stranglehold on a comprehensive science of networks, nor is that likely to happen. Rather, any deep understanding of the structure of real networks can come only through a genuine marriage of ideas and data that have lain dispersed across the intellectual spectrum, each piece

> of the puzzle with its own fascinating history and insights, but none the key to the puzzle itself. As with jigsaw puzzles, the key is the way in which all the parts interlock to form a single unified picture.[5]

While the theorists are fitting the pieces together, burgeoning real-world digital enterprises are causing the networks to take over more and more aspects of our lives. It is not necessary for us to follow the speculation in full detail to get an increasingly good idea of how networks work, nor to gain insight into their significant value in coping with our changing world. This chapter is an overview of the practical role of networks.

My reading revealed that my own insight that networks are a common factor among many fields was not a breakthrough for humankind. The same idea had been popping up in a lot of other places, described by the words *network, net,* and *web* interchangeably as a basic structure found in the many fields Watts mentioned. What does it mean, you may ask, for networks to be an integral part of these sorts of things. Before listing some useful things to know that we learn from net structure, we will look at actual networks in the cosmos, language, and elephants.

In the cosmic sense, a network is the biggest thing there is, as I saw from an observer chair in the Hayden Sphere. As the twentieth century waned, the Rose Center for Earth and Space was built on the spot where the half dome-topped Hayden Planetarium had nestled since 1935 on the grounds of the American Museum of Natural History in Manhattan. The Rose Center is clad in a transparent box made of nearly an acre of glass. Inside the gleaming cube the eighty-seven-foot diameter Hayden Sphere is suspended. To those of us who recall the old planetarium, the visual effect of the new one is a jolt of wonder that somehow the Hayden has risen out of the Earth, and now hovers, glistening and inviting. When it opened to the public in 2000, its director Neil de Grasse Tyson said that the goal in developing the new center was to "take the most fundamental questions we could ask about how the universe works and design and conceive the exhibitry around that."[6]

The centerpiece for the display of what is to be learned at the Rose Center is in the theater that fills the top half of the Hayden Sphere. There the supercomputer of the Digital Dome System spews enormous amounts of astronomical information into visual simulations. When our

Milky Way is displayed by the Digital Galaxy software, the real location of every star and nebula is calculated thirty times a second. Twenty-eight central processing units, with two terabytes of storage, can process fourteen gigabytes of data. I have now seen three of the enormously popular twenty-minute shows prepared by the Hayden. Each of them is wonderful, but I will never forget the first one, "Passport to the Universe."

My excitement about the first show stems from a single idea I learned from it about networks. When you pay for admission to the show, you are issued a passport for travel to the farthest distances of the known universe. As darkness falls inside the dome, you hear the narrator, Tom Hanks, describe the trip. The adventure begins as you travel through and beyond our solar system and soon are enveloped in the full magnificence of the Digital Galaxy's visualization prowess. Then you move on past more distant galaxies, back farther and farther in time, as Hanks explains you must do to achieve distance. The end of the journey is a depiction of the farthest extent of the known universe. When we arrived at the edge of what is known and I saw what was projected across the grand expanse of the Hayden Sphere's ceiling, my skin and my mind both tingled. The entire image, from horizon to horizon in every direction was a web. What I saw was network structure portraying the biggest known entity: everything.

Elsewhere at the turn of the twenty-first century networks were being investigated in all sorts of places. Tiny things like cells and molecules function as networks to maintain life, and so do food chains that sustain life on a macro scale. Our relations with other people are networks as well, and so is our language. A July 2002 article in *Nature* reports the findings of a group at Arizona State University, Tempe, led by Adilson Motter: "The semantic links between English words make the thesaurus a 'small world,' much as the network of human social interactions connects us all by six degrees of separation. . . . The researchers expect languages other than English to have the same properties, even if their syntactic structure is very different."[7] The same article broaches the notion that our thoughts are networks, too. Continuing from *Nature*:

> The researchers think that the network structure of a language probably has its origins in the nature of cognition and memory. It is not surprising

> that language is highly clustered, as we remember things associatively—by grouping similar concepts together. This makes it easier for us to retrieve related words from our memory. . . . It remains to be seen whether searching our memories for a particular word really entails wandering mentally along links in the network.[8]

As the twenty-first century began, nets that I have dubbed "dynamic" were also beginning to be used on the ground as the following example with elephants illustrates.

Hansa turned a ton at the beginning of 2003. The pampered little elephant took more than two years to reach 2,000 pounds from the 235 she weighed when she was born at the Seattle Zoo in November 2000. At her ton weight, she was still a child, though, who will eventually weigh around 7,000 pounds when she finishes growing up over the next decade. Hansa's life unfolds virtually online at zoo.org,[9] the website of her Seattle Zoo home. Her story presented there includes the adventures of her mother Chai's road trip to the Dickerson Park Zoo in Springfield, Missouri, to meet and mate with Hansa's father Onyx, Hansa's birth, and lots of continually updated facts and photos. Hansa is a node in several networks—networks of children who enjoy studying elephants, networks of conservationists and scientists devoted to pachyderms, networks of zookeepers who see her as a helpful attraction of support to zoos, and people like me who just enjoy looking in on animals.

There are many other excellent web projects featuring elephants. A favorite of mine, which I have been following for several years, is called Elephants of Cameroon and is now part of FieldTripEarth.com. The following is an entry describing attempts to locate a previously collared wild bull elephant named Joseph, reported from the ground in Cameroon by Dr. Mike Loomis, chief veterinarian at the North Carolina Zoological Park:

> When we arrived at Joseph's last location, Desire tried to locate the collar using the VHF receiver, but could not pick up a signal. This seemed very strange, so the group spread out and began searching the area. Jason called Mark (who is in North Carolina) on the satellite phone to see if by an off-chance we had received any new location data for Joseph. We had!

> The new position was 1.7 kilometers south of our current position, well out of the margin of error of our location data. The only explanation was that the collar had moved. . . . When we arrived at the new location, Desire was once again unable to get a VHF signal, but it was obvious that a large elephant had been in the area very recently. All signs of human activity in the area were at least six months old, so we found this very encouraging. With all the evidence at hand, it appeared that Joseph had not been poached![10]

The Elephants of Cameroon project, like the Hansa pages, forms a node in many networks. Conservationist connect into it, many school teachers and children follow the elephants and exchange emails with the scientists, and elephant aficionados in general enjoy the site.

After reading here about Hansa and Joseph, you might go online and check them out. If you do so, you will travel through the elephant pages on a dynamic net you create and control. The ideas you will get from your visit will be unique to you. You will be connecting nodes dynamically, like a spider spinning its web, from node to another as you click on a new page or image. You will be experiencing network structure. When any person in either Hansa's or Joseph's networks enters either website, a dynamic net will form in the pattern of the visitor's activity. If the person is a conservationist she might look at Hansa's latest physical report and read the good news that Joseph's trail had been found and perhaps forward a link or two to a fellow scientist. Her dynamic net would be a ripple of activity across several interconnected networks of ideas and communication. Ten years ago, the conservationist would have had to read separate newsletters from the Seattle and North Carolina zoos and write and mail a letter to her scientist friends to approximate something like what she could do in a few moments by using her dynamic nets. The dynamic net that connected Joseph's radio collar to the data center in North Carolina and then by satellite to the trackers on the ground in Cameroon could not have occurred until very late in the twentieth century.

Before dynamic nets were possible, the conservationist, or the birder described in the last chapter, could have picked up the phone and called someone to report information. A simple linear connection between two people, two nodes, is not a network. A conference call where several people are connected by telephone to each other simultaneously is a simple network, and we could think of such a call as a dynamic net. When different sorts of networks are interconnected, dynamic nets get more interesting. In the example of the elephants, networks include web pages, satellite communication, radio collars, digital images, and human expression (the diary recording the Joseph tracking).

What I realized on my train ride was that all the complex activities of galaxies, grammar, and elephant tracking all formed networks. Their networking is what they have in common, and what we know about the network helps us know about galaxies, grammar, and elephants—and about a great deal of all reality.

Recently a lot has been learned about networks, and ongoing discoveries are being made in a broad variety of academic and applied fields. What awes me is that we have been given a totally new and elegant way to visit, travel, and connect ideas and transactions within many of the networks and—even more awesomely—among them! With a few quick clicks, I can compare the nesting pattern of whooper swans with the birthing habitats of elephants and in doing so access the most erudite of the experts on those subjects. Dynamic nets are the integrating tool of digital content. They are utterly new and I think there is no way to overestimate their importance.

TEN USEFUL THINGS TO KNOW ABOUT NETWORKS

Professor Strogatz has pointed out that by pulling back far enough in our perspective of networks, we can begin to see generalities among them:

> Network theory is concerned with the relationships between individuals, the patterns of interactions. The precise nature of individuals is downplayed, or even suppressed, in hopes of uncovering deeper laws. A network theorist will look at any system of interlinked components and see an abstract pattern of dots connected by lines. It's that pattern that matters, the architecture of relationships, not the identities of the dots themselves. Viewed from these lofty heights, many networks, seemingly unrelated, begin to look the same.[11]

In the current, early stages of network studies, there is considerable complexity and definitely a sprinkling of chaos about exactly what we understand so far. Still, from the perspective Strogatz describes, significant pieces of order have been teased out and these are beginning to give us some rules and tools. To give you an idea of what these are, ten useful things we know about networks are explained here. They are my own selections and observations. They are not an expert's primer on networks, but I think they are instructive. The chapter concludes by returning to dynamic nets as a way humans can usefully deal with the networked world in which we increasingly find ourselves. I use the ten points and the dynamic net implementation in later chapters to discuss what networks can tell us about frustrating terrorism, the new ways we conduct business, expressing ideas, interfacing knowledge, and doing something fundamental about the failure of education.

These are new ideas and not proven in any systematic way. Please read them in that spirit and add your own. The authors in the network sciences regularly include in what they write their hope that their readers will pick up and continue the quest to understand and harness network ideas. When I finished his book, *Linked*, I sent an e-mail to Professor Barabási thanking him for introducing me to so many interesting ideas. He was good enough to respond, and said, "The hope of *Linked* was to make people like you think about networks, and understand many of the network related problems around us."[12] I offer the following in the same spirit.

1. The Structure of a Network Is Not a Hierarchy[13]

Although they are nonlinear with no way to go up or down, from their beginnings the Internet and World Wide Web have had hierarchies forced on them from every quarter—and the result has never been pretty. The structure of a hierarchy is like a tree or the favorite organizational tool of lawyers and textbook writers, the outline. You branch out by making a big point that has sub-points which in turn have their sub-sub-points. You go from I to A, to 1, to a—dividing a subject into ever greater levels of detail. Things are only allowed to go up and down and to ramify (Latin for branch) splitting into smaller parts. Things cannot go sideways and cannot come back to touch themselves. There is no equality. There is no feedback except by going up and down the same route.

The Internet and World Wide Web have exposed the difficulties and folly of using hierarchies to organize almost all real subjects. Digital technologies and the Internet have introduced a new web/net medium of organizing things. It follows logically that a networked system of organization is appropriate for interfacing our networked world. Hierarchies are clumsy relics that belong on the antique shelf with quill pens, typewriters and carbon paper. We will return to the folly of hierarchies several times in the chapters that follow. Perhaps the most important insight will be that although it is routine for people to use hierarchies to organize ideas and control other people, we now know there is a better way available.

There is a smugness hanging around among those who persist with linear databases and tree-shaped web materials that it is just fine to stuff everything into a hierarchy because it is simpler and cheaper. But it is not fine at all. Here is the fundamental reason they are wrong, in Strogatz's words:

> Whenever nonlinear elements are hooked together in gigantic webs, the wiring diagram has to matter. It's a basic principle: Structure always affects function. The structure of social networks affects the spread of information and disease; the structure of the power grid affects the stability of power transmission. The same must be true for species in an ecosystem, companies in the global marketplace, cascades of enzyme reactions in living cells. The layout of the web must profoundly shape its dynamics.[14]

Bottom line: Very little of reality can be validly reflected in a tree or outline; hierarchies are false reflectors. The shoehorning of the webs of meaning that compose academic subjects makes learning them far more difficult, if not impossible, as we will see in chapter 7.

2. "Networks Are the Skeleton of Complexity"[15]

The title of this point is a quotation from Albert-László Barabási. In recent decades a large number of very smart people have been caught up in the fascinating sciences and philosophies that investigate and speculate on how order arises from chaos and complexity. There are those who are deeply disquieted by the considerable apparent chaos of the times in which we live. Ancient traditions have crumbled, transforming technologies are set loose in the world, globalism is mixing things into new and incomprehensible gumbos. Is all lost for humankind? I am heartened to learn that order does indeed rise out of chaos. We have learned in recent years that order from within complexity is a network, a web—that networks are the skeleton of that order. That new message of hope has deep implications for politics, sociology, business, art, academics, and learning. It will be part of many discussions in the pages ahead. Understanding it is a practical matter because as you cast your dynamic nets to say and do activities, you are forming in the chaos skeletons that become fleshed out with your purposes and meaning. That is not spooky stuff; it is exactly what the birder did when he reported the whooper swan building her nest.

3. Sync Emerges from Complexity with Webbed Connections

Acting on no instructions, the pendulums of two clocks, the 10,000 pacemaker cells of your heart, thousands of fireflies at dusk on a hillside in Malaysia, and the entire audience in an Eastern Europe concert hall spontaneously swing, fire, flash, and clap in perfect unison. The gamut of spontaneous synchronizers ranges from mechanical things like clocks that are not even alive to the most intelligent inhabitants of Earth, us. Even atoms willingly emit light waves in sync, giving us the laser.

The investigations of sync, which began in the seventeenth century when Christiaan Huygens noticed the pendulums of two clocks in his bedroom synchronizing themselves, have shown the phenomenon to be common and a relatively simple example of spontaneous order emerging from complexity. Why does syncing occur? Strogatz suggests in his explanation of the sync of our pacemaker cells that 10,000 cells acting as one may be a more dependable mechanism for assuring that the right signal is sent every time than relying on a single signaler cell. In synchronizing for the firing event, a few cells that are too slow, others too fast, and some that fail altogether would not prevent the vast majority, like the fireflies on the Malay hillside, from firing as one. When I read this idea in Strogatz, it gave me a new way to look at why democracy and government by majority of individuals has proved to be the platform for golden ages in history. We will return to this idea in the next chapter.

Watts, whose study of the synchronized chirping of crickets led him into breakthrough discoveries, says of synchrony, "Like so many of the questions in this story, this one is essentially about the emergence of some global behavior from the interactions of many individuals. Synchronization of oscillators just happens to be a particularly simple and well-defined version of emergence. . . ."[16] The emergence of a small group of synchronized clappers in a concert hall can result in the whole hall emerging to clap in unison. The connections among the clappers and clocks, among the crickets and fireflies, and among your pacemaker cells are networks.

4. The Structure of a Network Is a Web That Supports Movement in All Directions

The fundamental structural rule that makes something a network is the connection of dots by lines—nodes and links. Anything that makes the pattern of a network more complicated than nodes and links is something added on and not part of the basic web structure. In terms of structure, every node is just a node and every link is just a link. The elements of a network are like a standard toy of my pre-electronics childhood, Tinkertoys. In case you are too young to know what they are: Tinkertoys have just two parts, a wheel with peg holes in its center and at intervals all the way around its curved outer surface and sticks that fit the holes to connect the wheels. A network is the same thing except a network's connector wheels (nodes) point outward in every direction and can accept an unlimited number of sticks (links). In network structure, at every node you can send an infinite number of links to other nodes, building outward in any and every direction creating a web of many different paths to follow from node to node inward, outward and back through a node in myriad different routes.

The Tinkertoy structure of networks is something like pulling back to the lofty view suggested by Strogatz, and emphasizes an important new way of looking at how things are and should be organized. Tinkertoys can help us to shake loose our practical preoccupation with hierarchies: which wheel is boss and which stick most important in a Tinkertoy network of connections? A net structure does not designate a boss and it does facilitate cooperation. I recently was chatting about this with a friend who has an MBA from Harvard and is a managing vice president of a major brokerage house. I told her there were no centers of power in a network and that might be a useful idea in a business structure. She clearly thought I was wrong, but she is a brilliant woman and listened quietly to my description of pacemaker cells in her heart spontaneously firing together at exactly the right time—somehow all acting together and getting it right every time. Her response was that actually her company was using a new plan of networking among a lot of people before accepting a new idea, rather than just letting her make a change. She said it seemed like more work for her, but it might be a good idea.

Government tyrannies, bureaucracies, militaries, corporate hierarchies, branches of academic knowledge, textbooks, and social clubs are habitually set up in hierarchies. I believe unfolding knowledge from the science and practice of networking gives us helpful new ways of tinkering with these structures and in some cases replacing them with networks.

Unlike in a hierarchy, in a network you cannot assign power to nodes. Your place in a hierarchy is defined as being above or below someone else. In a web (network) you are only connected. This relationship is being discovered in new places all the time and appears to be one of the most successful forms of organization. Food webs found in nature balance and recycle resources among mammals, birds, reptiles, fish, insects, and all sorts of microscopic creatures. The network of who eats whom emerges from the complexity of the ecology—no one is in charge. We will wonder in the chapters that follow how much more balanced human affairs could be if we do more networking and less order-giving.

In a different kind of benefit, the web structure of digital nets has given us a marvelous new form of expression. It allows us to form a matrix that mirrors an idea. Chapter 5 delves into the new medium of network structure that the Internet provides for richly interfacing ideas.

5. Nets Clarify Relationships and Let Us Experience Context

Once again to beat up on hierarchies: they are really lousy at creating or allowing context. When you organize something within a hierarchy, the only context available is the hierarchy. In contrast to the rigidity of I, A, 1, a, the web structure of a net is wonderfully pliable. The hierarchical outline demands that you dissect and prioritize pieces of your topic and put them into a tree-shape. A web, on the other hand, will conform to the natural shape of your subject. A web will also let you connect a single idea to several other ideas, which is not possible in an outline. If that sounds theoretical, remember what happens in the Dewey Decimal Classification System, a library hierarchy standard. When 500 and 600 divide, natural sciences and mathematics go into one bucket and technology (applied sciences) goes into another, leaving a limbo for many subjects like digital biology. At the juncture for 700 and 800, arts are separated from literature and rhetoric, never again to meet. No literary art will be found in the 700s. Of course these separations are necessary in a brick-and-mortar library because the librarian must know on which shelf to place each book for it to be findable by a reader. In the virtual world of the Internet, a work of writing or art can be placed in every category where it belongs. I realize library science has addressed difficulties of hierarchical cataloging, but the solutions do not approach the elegance of virtual redundancy and unlimited linking.

In chapters 6 and 7 we will explore virtual context further. I think this stunning new power to organize within context may be the most important intellectual gift of the Internet. The quotation at the beginning of this chapter from Watts mentioned "a genuine marriage of ideas and data that have lain dispersed across the intellectual spectrum. . . ."[17] The context powers of web structure facilitate merging dispersed ideas in ways that cannot happen in the brick-and-mortar world. Think of a library table stacked with related books compared to a web page with interactive connections to the same ideas that the books on the table contain.

Context—or to be more to the point, broken context—is a cause and misery of the education system, severely stunting curricula and standards. Chapter 7 will explore this in depth and point to web structure as the way to harness the pedagogical wonders of virtual context. What can happen is a beautiful thing. In a hierarchy you are always under things and over things. In a web, you are always in the center. In learning within a web you are in two centers! The first one is your own position within your own understanding, in touch through some links with what you already know and reaching out through others to touch what you are ready to learn. The second center you are in is that of the content of what you are studying. Wherever you move within that content you are at the node at the center of the relevant context. Although both centers are still primitive at this stage of the development in cyberspace, they are becoming more and more precise and pristine as the Internet matures. Chapter 6 explores these processes in detail.

6. A Common Type of Network Form Is into Small Worlds[18]

Six degrees of separation catches the imagination. When I mentioned the idea to the seventh-graders I was teaching once a week, most of them had heard of it. One of the boys responded with delight: "I am only separated by six steps from every person on Earth!" So the popular idea goes. Is this so? How could it be so? The answer is: It's the nets. Clearly in a net with regular steps from knot to knot, leaving holes for water but too small for a fish to pass through, a knot at one side of the net would be separated by many more than six knots from one at the opposite side. Nets with such regular steps could not explain the closeness of humans to one another. In 1998 Strogatz and Watts came up with a network pattern where the average steps of separation are very small—not exactly the famed six, but even smaller sometimes and other times a bit larger. Strogatz writes:

> The most important result of the simulations was that over a broad intermediate range of rewiring, the model networks were very clustered and very small at the same time. That peculiar combination was new to mathematics. . . . We dubbed the network with this pair of seemingly contradictory properties "small-world networks," in homage to the same duality that seems so paradoxical about human connectedness: We move in tight circles yet we are all bound together by remarkably short chains.[19]

I grew up in El Paso, Texas, and visit family and old friends there about once a year. Almost all the people I know in El Paso know each other. I have lived in New York City for many years where I also have friends who not only know me, but also know each other. Through me, all of my El Paso friends are separated by one degree from any one of my New York friends and by two degrees from every one of my New York friends who know the friend to whom I introduce my first New York friend. Obviously, the minimization of separation works the other way too: my New York friends are linked to my El Paso friends by a remarkably short chain—me. The surprising connectedness that Stanley Milgram stumbled onto in the 1960s experiments that started the six degrees of separation mystery had not been explained mathematically until the work of Strogatz and Watts in 1998. But more was revealed by the strange new networks than the linking of individual people. It has turned out that the small-world networks are all over the place, connecting things living and dead, large and small, real and virtual. The Internet is one of them and so are electrical power grids and the nervous system of the *C. elegans* nematode. These and many other real-world manifestations of connectedness have the characteristics of small-world networks, including clusters and hubs from which weak connectors link. The small-world nets are elucidating diverse subjects and many small-world projects are under way. We will come back often in coming chapters to this central subject in the new science of networks.

7. Scale-Free Net Structure Elevates Winners in a Small-World Network

When Barabási and his team at the Notre Dame University Department of Physics discovered that small-world networks do not operate on a bell curve, they called the nets scale-free.[20] The term has become widely used among those who study networks. There are several phrases that refer to what happens in a scale-free network: the rich get richer, the law of the few, the 80/20 rule, popularity is attractive, and in mathematics the power law that produces a very fat tail on a graph instead of a bell curve. What all of these words refer to has practical implications that I think will change how we use the Internet, lift the curtain on a brand-new stage of art and interpretation, and transform our wimpy school curricula and standards into potent tools for learning.

In the bell curve of IQ fame, there is a smooth rise upward from the few geniuses in the 160+ range up to those with the 100 average IQ at the top of the bell shape, which is completed by a downward curve to least intelligent few in the 30- group. If IQ statistically followed the power law, there might be a handful of people with an IQ of 1,000, a few more ranging through the hundreds and then everybody else would be at something like 50 and below. The curve would start high up, drop precipitously, and then extend a long way at a low level. The Internet looks like that, with a few sites receiving a huge number of hits, such as Yahoo and Amazon. A graph including the big sites and all the other Web pages out there would start very high and then drop precipitously and extend at a very low level for a very long time, representing the billions of Web pages that receive only a few hits.

The first time I noticed the 80/20 rule was in the spring of 2000. Although I had never heard of the power law, I found its footprint in the only metrics the companies that owned it ever bothered to wring out of HomeworkCentral.com while I led the content team. I had waged a battle with the leaders of the company that had just bought our collection of learning links about how many study pages were needed to serve the requests of our clientele, which at that point represented four million page views a month. The new owners said 15,000 links would be plenty. We already had about 150,000 links divided into 35,000 subjects ranging from plane geometry to mouse anatomy to steam engines to the sonnets of Shakespeare. For one week in May 2000 our tech team kept track of how many hits each subject received. The results showed that about 20 percent got about 80 percent of the page views, but almost every other subject received a small number of hits. There were a few giants: arithmetic and a couple of the sciences. The metrics followed the power law perfectly.

My hunch about scale-free networks is that they appear as a reflection of utility and thought. I think they are an enormously important indicator that small-world scale-free nets offer powerful possibilities for harnessing the complexities of the Internet, of swarming people in the newly connected age, of the digital expressive medium and of the interfacing of knowledge. We need less to organize these arenas of complexity than to travel and enhance the paths of the networks they already contain. In chapter 6 we will return to the scale-free principle to discuss it as a way to move past search engine frustrations.

Finally, a small-world scale-free platform offers a virtual net of useful knowledge used in common by everyone on Earth—which will end any educational divide, digital, or otherwise. If the prospect of a great global commons for knowledge seems a futurist fantasy, it is a bit of a jolt to realize that the so-called massively multiplayer online games have exactly that already, as described in this newspaper report: "these games are really only about the relationships among the people who play them. . . . Where thousands of people simultaneously occupy a common (if vast) virtual environment, those relationships are real."[21]

8. Structural Nets and Functional Nets Are Not the Same

In the first chapter, I quoted Barabási's distinction between these two roles in genes. In heredity their key contribution is structural information that is encoded with instructions that they pass on to an organism's offspring. That has been known for a long time. But this is new, as Barabasi put it: "Genes also play an important *functional* role as members of a complex cellular network. This functional role is apparent only in the dynamic context in which an individual gene interacts with many other cellular components."[22]

Here is Strogatz's explanation of the same idea:

> Traditionally, the genome has been viewed as a blueprint for the construction of proteins, which in turn act as the building blocks for the cellular structures and molecular machines essential for life. But today we see that metaphor is too static, too linear, a vestige of the assembly-line mentality of an earlier era. Some of the most important genes (the so-called regulatory genes) code for proteins that alter the activity of other genes, turning them on or off, forming circuits and feedback loops. The genome starts to seem less like a blueprint and more like a computer. The functioning of this computer—and its malfunctioning when cells turn cancerous—will not be deciphered until we understand the logic of gene networks.[23]

So it is that the function of the genes is a matter of dynamic nets generated by the genes themselves! We learn here from the nature of life that a network not only is a structure and a container, but it also can be a way of doing things. Things that are done by your computer are essentially dynamic nets by this insight. So are many things we do in our interactions with other people. An idea is a dynamic network as you think about it. As set out in chapter 1, handhelds possessed by all will equip each person with dynamic net capacity within our new digital world. In the same vein, things are different when everyone is heard from than when there is a static instruction and no interaction.

9. The Net Medium Richly Interfaces Gestalts and Isomorphs

The Altamira caves in Spain contain images of bison painted on the walls about 15,000 years ago. The pictures clearly convey the idea of a bison, including its appearance, power, and movement. The artists used multimedia to express the bison: the texture and relief of the rock surface, folds in the rock for key lines in the image and colors of yellow, red and brown earth, and blacks from manganese and charcoal. Multimedia in the digital world forms an extensive pallet of line, color, photography, motion, sound, and interaction. Multimedia students and artists have access to all the work of the ages, from Altamira to a photo of this morning's sunrise. Yet none of what I have mentioned so far is the big new thing in expression. What is very new in expression is the nets. Chapter 5 describes networks as a tool of expression. A net's talent for mirroring meaning stems from the ability of a digital web to be configured to mirror reality virtually. The implications of digital nets as a medium of expression are enormous for communication, creativity, and learning.

10. Epidemics Cascade across Nets

The new network science is making an important contribution to understanding and stopping epidemics of disease and computer viruses. In small-world scale-free nets, bad bugs can hop a ride on short-cut connectors, quickly and dangerously spreading through clusters and hubs. Optimist that I am, that says to me that good bugs can spread too. The more positive side of epidemics has potent implications for marketing and learning. We will return to the topic in chapters 4 and 7.

The cascading across nets is a cousin of context. The openness of the nodes and links and their congregations at hubs that support the flow of an epidemic also makes a wonderful platform for echoing the real-world relationships of ideas and events. Whereas our old enemy the hierarchy is seldom more than a simplistic abstraction of the real world, the complexity of a net can be a closely resembling reflection.

The mobility of cell phones, and soon of the handheld, multitalented computers, is changing the technologies of communication from fixed trees and networks into unfixed and dynamic nets. We will touch on this in future chapters.

DYNAMIC NETS GIVE US INTERACTIVITY AND MORE THAN JUST ACCESS

The handheld device that is advocated and predicted in this book allows the individual who possesses it to become a participant in the unfolding world sketched in this chapter by the ten useful things to know about networks. It means everyone can be heard. There are two other factors that complete the picture of a person who is sending dynamic nets into the digital milieu.

First, dynamic nets are not passive as the media that we have been used to using; they are interactive. The difference is the same as listening to someone play a clarinet and playing it yourself. The difference is the same as watching a recreational video and hiking along the actual Appalachian Trail. Our Internet industry is barely beginning to implement the powers of interactivity. The focus in most websites is still a step removed from engaging a visitor; instead, the gurus continue to focus on letting visitors use a site rather than being there. Usability and participation are not the same thing. We are on the cusp of truly engaging Internet content, as we will explore in chapter 5.

Second, using dynamic nets is more than just access. Access, in fact, is one of the least facile aspects of using the Internet and cell phones today. It is hard to find things. For those of us in the senior generation, thumb-typing just seems like too much to have to do after finally getting competent on a keyboard. Twenty- and thirty-somethings are getting a taste of what the seniors went through when they had to lay down their pens and learn to type. Most of the people who truly understand that using the grand new milieu of networks are younger than twelve. Exceptions are Frank Newman, director of the Futures Project at Brown University, and Xerox chief scientist John Seely Brown. In a January 2003 interview, Newman talked about the how the youngest generation approaches things:

> In a recent communication, John Seely Brown said that people keep talking about students being technologically literate but that, to 12-year-olds, technology literacy is not the main concern. What matters to them is that technology is how you talk to people, how you meet people, and how you deal with people. They play computer games that feature fabulous simulation. They learn intuitively. We, on the other hand, are text-based learners. If we want someone to learn a concept, then we ask him or her to read the following 270 pages and be prepared for a discussion of the text during the next class. That is not how today's 12-year-olds learn; in fact, it is not how they do anything. They plunge right in, and they are very successful when they do so.[24]

Using the Internet for access would be finding the 270 pages mentioned above, and reading them on a monitor screen or printing them and using the printout like a book. That certainly would be access. Already the text of a very high percentage of what has ever been printed is available on the Internet. In addition, a lot of important formerly printed material such as the most recent Congressional Directory, genome facts and stock market details, are available *only* through the new network milieu. Access is a great strength of the world developing around us but considering it primary boxes in our thinking and keeps us from knowing other more useful and important things about networks. I risk belaboring this point for a reason. If you are among those who say—out loud or to yourself—"I would rather just go look it up in a book," you are not making a choice between equal or even similar options. I urge you to join the twelve-year-olds: plunge into the nets! You will be successful when you do.

NOTES

1. Albert-Lászlő Barabási, *Linked* (Cambridge, Mass.: Perseus, 2002), 225–26.

2. Steven Strogatz, *Sync: The Emerging Science of Spontaneous Order* (New York: Hyperion, 2003).

3. Duncan J. Watts, *Six Degrees: The Science of a Connected Age*. (New York: W.W. Norton, 2003).

4. Barabási, *Linked*.

5. Watts, *Six Degrees*, 68.

6. Online movie from the Rose Center, www.amnh.org/rose/animations/tyson-landmark.mpg [accessed 23 March 2003].

7. *Nature, Scienceupdate*, "Small World Networks," 2 July 2002. www.nature.com/nsu/020701/020701–2.html [accessed April 14, 2003].

8. *Nature*.

9. Seattle Zoo, "Elephant Home," www.zoo.org/chai/site/main.htm [accessed 6 May 2003].

10. Mike Loomis, "Elephant Encounters in Djembe," Online diary, 22 April 2003, www.fieldtripearth.org/article.xml?id=871 [accessed 23 April 2003].

11. Strogatz, *Sync*, 231–32.

12. Breck personal correspondence, 7 March 2003.

13. As this manuscript goes to final typesetting, the paperback edition of Professor Barabási's book *Linked* has been released. He has added an "Afterlink" in which he describes the discovery over the past year of hierarchical modularity in networks. How does this square with my assertion that the structure of a network is not a hierarchy?

In the first place, it does not change my conviction concerning anything I say in these pages about hierarchies as they have been thrust upon the Internet. What I am referring to are content arranged in pre-Internet outlines, categorizations and descending databases. Secondly, the hierarchy of modularity is a structure among units that are not themselves essentially hierarchies—they are omnidirectionally interconnected nodes forming networks, not the branching trees of a hierarchy. Within those network the modules' tasks are carried on by the interaction of nodes not constricted by an internal hierarchy. Much more will be learned, but I remain convinced that repositioning non-network outlines into webs is at best very messy business; Albert-Laszlo' Barabási, *Linked* (New York: Perseus, 2003), 227–38.

14. Strogatz, *Sync*, 236.

15. Barabási, *Linked*, 225.

16. Watts, *Six Degrees*, 31.

17. Watts, *Six Degrees*, 68.

18. A textbook definition of small-world networks: Roughly speaking, small-world networks are equilibrium networks, which are made from regular lattices by connecting pairs of vertices chosen at random. In fact, this is a superposition of a regular lattice and classical random graph. Even a very small number of such shortcuts, which do not change the local properties (a high clustering typical of a regular lattice), already produce values of the average shortest-path length, which are typical of classical random graphs. S. N. Dorogovtsev and J. F. F. Mendes, *Evolution of Networks: From Biological Nets to the Internet and WWW* (Oxford University Press, 2003), 22–23.

19. Strogatz, 242–43.

20. A textbook definition of scale-free networks: "Networks growing under the mechanism of preferential linking due to Barabási and Albert. Roughly speaking, these are growing networks where new edges become attached to vertices preferentially. By definition, this means that more connected vertices have a better chance to get new connections." S. N. Dorogovtsev and J. F. F. Mendes, *Evolution of Networks: From Biological Nets to the Internet and WWW* (Oxford University Press, 2003), 23.

21. Seth Schiesel, "Voyager to a Strange Planet," New York Times Online, [accessed June 12, 2003]

22. Barabási, 183.

23. Strogatz, 231.

24. *Vision.* January/February 2003, http://ts.mivu.org/default.asp?show=article&id=1003 [accessed May 11, 2003].

3

A NETWORK TO TERMINATE TERROR: MENDING THE HUMAN WEB

> Human history is an evolution from simple sameness to diversity and then toward complex structures. Our remotest ancestors lived in simple, small groups, spoke only a few languages, and pursued a narrow range of survival strategies in East Africa. As groups spread out across the world, broader cultural variety emerged—more languages, differing toolkits, more social complexity. But the trend toward cultural differentiation did not last. Through the growth of interactive webs, best practices spread, diversity declined, and complexity became the rule—the new uniformity. Societies that resisted were wiped out. At present human society is one huge web of cooperation and competition, sustained by massive flows of information and energy. How long these flows, and this web, might last is an open question.[1]
>
> —J. R. McNeill and William H. McNeill

The repercussions of the 9/11 attacks cascaded across the world for weeks and months and still dominate planet politics even more pervasively than have empires and totalitarian dictators in past eras. A thing we have come to call terrorism is affecting everyone in a consistently negative manner. The amount of anguish and effort it has already used up is phenomenal. It has not been at all clear what a victory against terror would be—how it could be truly terminated. Certainly we will not be able to return to the way things were on September 10, 2001. Return to innocence is never possible. Humpty Dumpty will not ever be really whole again, even if he is masterfully glued back together.

It is not hard to become very discouraged, and to wonder whether the web of humanity is tattering. We know that at least to some degree it is. American military superpower, complete with shock and awe, is the only sizable deterrent to aggression of global scale, and it is minimally effective against the havoc caused by either a suicide bomber or a culture long accustomed to the ignorance and licenses enforced by tyranny. But there is optimism to be found in a very different vein: it is an approach that I believe will be the key to ending the tattering of the web of humanity and will erect the platform of a new global golden age. That approach is to see to it that all individuals are connected interactively into the nets. This is something I have thought for several years was critical step that would bring an end to ignorance, and I have written about it, both before and after 9/11. This book adds to the pivotal worth of hearing from everyone the promise that doing so will terminate terror. Many of us are connected, but there are billions we cannot hear yet. Network sciences teaches, I believe, that their participation will form a new kind of human complexity from which, the theories indicate, will come a new and better sort of order. A certain result, it seems clear to me, will be the termination of terror. I know that is a big idea, but it is also a completely new option—worth a try in this reeling world.

Five years ago, to support my confidence in the individual I would have used arguments from ideas that go back to the roots of liberty in ancient Athens, eighteenth-century England and the American Revolution. Those beliefs uphold the sovereignty of the individual and the unalienable rights bestowed equally to each person by the Creator. I would also have argued that freedom of the individual has been the historical setting that has proven to cause golden ages. These are superb points, which I believe are correct and will always apply. But I am also aware that they are only one theory and that it is based on what many would say is too much faith in the individual. Plato, for one, thought the ideal way for people to be governed was to make a philosopher king sovereign, giving him all the power and letting him make all the key decisions. There remain those who think Karl Marx had it right in the equal sharing of possessions, in spite of the disastrous, corrupted experiments with communism in twentieth-century, Russia, China, North Korea, Cuba, and elsewhere. Others still are convinced that the placement of sufficient sovereignty in a world government—the core vision of the founders of the League of Nations and the United Nations—is the solution to the world's troubles, if we can just get the powers balanced.

The twentieth-century frustrations and failures from the endlessly exploding political chaos are paralleled by the failures over and over of those of us who have seen literacy and education as the solution to the woes of the world. Our thinking has been that ignorance is the root of all evil. Adam did not know that he was doing something really bad when he ate the apple. The snake fooled Eve, after all. My point here is not theological. The fact is that we still do not know if overcoming ignorance will overcome evil because we have failed miserably at overcoming ignorance. My guess is that eradicating ignorance will be tantamount to eradicating terror. The good news is that we are going to find out if I am right. But we delay the process by continuing to use, over and over, the failed methods of twentieth-century education.

Do we have to suck it up and try these same things again, retuning to them and seeing if we can make them succeed? Will we be occupied in the decades ahead as Rudyard Kipling describes in these familiar lines: If you can "watch the things you gave your life to, broken, And stoop and build 'em up with worn-out tools. . . ."[2]? Kipling tells us it is manly to do so, but we also know it is dreary business. I think we have a more hopeful and exciting place to work on a new solution, which is something that will recalibrate human relations in natural and wonderful ways. As J. R. McNeill and William H. McNeill say in the opening quotation of this chapter, humanity is an interactive web—a network. Very recent insights into the principles of networks give us guidelines for improving the health of the human web to the benefit of every node—of each person in the network. I think we will learn that the more individuals who are participating in the human web the healthier it is. The new way we can make each person a participant is to see to it that every individual everywhere has a handheld interactive device connected into the new meshed nets of our digital era.

Just as we find ourselves badly needing something new to guide our world rebuilding efforts, along has come a fresh set of ideas based in the unfolding understanding of networks. The bottom line of the new insight is this: there seems to be more to fear from the chaos caused by the order enforced by tyrannies (say, the condition of Baghdad under Saddam Hussein's control, or the economy of Castro's Cuba) than there is from the order that will emerge from the complexity of connectivity. The most marvelously rich complexity imaginable is that of humanity. I find it impossible to believe that enriching the network among us will make things worse.

I know that my opinion is the gut reaction of an optimist as well as my faith in the individual poking through. But the networks reinforce my positive view. Like most people throughout the ages, I also hold out no real hope that Plato's philosopher king will ever be found, and am convinced that even the rare benevolent dictator usually makes a mess of things. To give you a peek at the flavor of fresh ideas from the nets, the synchronization of 10,000 pacemaker cells in your heart keeps it beating correctly because evolution chose a democracy to make the decisions instead of choosing one kingpin neuron to do it. Concerning the pacemaker bundle of neurons, sync scientist Strogatz points out, "Of course, democracy raises its own problems. Somehow the cells have to coordinate their firings; if they send conflicting signals, the heart becomes deranged."[3] The global derangement set off on 9/11 is an indication of tatters in the human web that both allow terrorists to develop and know not how to contain and eliminate them. The net-related new science of spontaneous synchronization may give us key clues to how human action will emerge to mend these flaws and is already a very useful analogy to the workings of the human web.

The idea of humanity forming a network of the sort the new network science probes is quite new, for the obvious reason that the science is new. It follows that the idea of a networks terminating terror is a new idea—something the would-be architects of world peace have never had on the list to try in the past. As I was working on this manuscript, a monthly mailing arrived from the History Book Club. One of the featured offerings was *The Human Web: A Bird's-eye View of World History*. It was written by a father-and-son team of distinguished historians and published early in 2003. I ordered the book and received it a few days later. The statement from its text that appears at the beginning of this chapter is printed in large letters on the back of the jacket. What the McNeills have written is an erudite primer on ways network theory apply in history, and I recommend it to you. My point in this chapter takes off from the McNeills' statement that "human society is one huge web." I suggest knowing that provides us with a completely new method for building humanity's future—a future that does not include terrorism. Human society is one huge web, but not everyone can be heard yet—and that is something we can change.

As later chapters will discuss, the potential benefits of connecting people by getting them interactive handhelds have many aspects. People will be connected to each other, to their economic enterprises, to the expression of ideas and to what is known, to entertainment, and to all sorts of other things. This will be a very different sort of connectivity from the media of the twentieth century, primarily because the individual with the handheld connection will be sovereign over what goes out and what comes in. Radio and television cast information broadly, but the person receiving their material has no way to interact except to turn the broadcast off or walk away. He cannot be heard. The choices of what to receive by broadcast are limited to the span of a radio or television dial. A person casting a dynamic net into the new medium of meshed nets has billions of choices of what to receive, increasingly powerful ways to manipulate what is contacted and multiplying choices of what dynamic net on any particular occasion to configure, use and share.

If every person on the planet owned a handheld, would every person on the planet adapt to casting dynamic nets and start doing so? The answer to that is yes, nearly everyone, if the response is similar to what it has been in the past two centuries to newspapers, telephones, radios, and televisions. Getting news, making a phone call, exchanging written messages, listening to audio, looking at video streams, storing information, and interacting with websites are all becoming activities that are a matter of using dynamic nets. The two-way media that arrived at the end of the nineteenth century bridged distance along a line of communication, by telegraph and telephone. The mass media of the twentieth century broadcast messages in one direction: at people. The dynamic medium of the nets interconnects everybody in every direction and puts every single node (person) equally in charge.

The remainder of this chapter is divided into two sections. The first is a parable of an Afghan boy named Abdul. It describes the arrival of handhelds into his family to provide a view of what the world will be like when everyone has handheld interactive connectivity into the nets. The second section looks at the ten useful things to know about networks that I use in several chapters, this time in terms of how they might undermine and terminate terrorism.

THE PARABLE OF ABDUL

Abdul Khaled was seven years old in 2001, living in the high Hindu Kush mountains of Afghanistan, when the first donkeys carrying humanitarian relief arrived through the snow-filled pass from the valley far below his home village. As the fifty or so people who lived in his little town crowded around, a man pulling items out of one of the little donkeys' packs called Abdul over and gave him a book. Abdul hurried back to his family's house and sat at the small table near the kitchen fire. He turned the pages of his new treasure to find pictures of animals, some of which were familiar, like the cows and horses. Others were new and exciting like the monkeys and dolphins. Four years later Abdul still has the book. It is, he figures, probably the only one he will ever own. He does not imagine a need for books for himself or, in the future, for his children. He can read any book that ever existed via the book-size handheld that he now carries with him. He can also travel virtually to husbandry sources for cows and horses and to the jungle and undersea habitats of monkeys and dolphins, learning far about the animals than books could convey.

We look in on Abdul at age eleven as he sits by the fire at the kitchen table in his village home. He has deployed a dynamic net to study chemistry. The net includes his own mind, a table of periodic elements at Los Alamos, a virtual experiment at MIT, and a whiteboard link to a mentor teacher in Kabul. He has also booted and keeps handy, as an icon on his handheld's screen, a collection of dictionaries from several Internet sources, which he does not need as often as he used to, but dips into now and then to verify the meaning of a word. Abdul's goal with his current work on chemistry is to take the online certification exam for the equivalent of college freshman chemistry before his twelfth birthday. That certification will qualify him to apply for a virtual apprenticeship in a project sponsored by Qatar's largest petroleum facility. Abdul is eager to become a chemist and belongs to a ChemWiz netgroup with members from twenty-seven countries. The group includes budding chemists, chemistry professors, and practicing chemists in the industry, all of whom activate dynamic nets to exchange ideas and enthusiasm online.

Abdul received his first handheld in the spring of 2004. He was among thirty Afghan children who were provided with the handhelds by a cooperative project between the Qatar petroleum company now sponsoring apprenticeships and a U.S. mobile device manufacturer. The original handheld was replaced a year later with a new model that had a larger screen for interfacing the Internet and which was by then being mass produced at a wholesale price of less than $200. When Abdul received his second handheld, it was part of the delivery of fifty, which provided every person in his village with a personal handheld. The $10,000 that paid for the fifty handhelds came from an international literacy foundation, which had recently switched all of its resources to the Global Handheld movement (see chapter 8).

When the donkey delivered the book to Abdul in 2001, there was no Internet access through the valleys of the Hindu Kush. WI-FI was still a trendy and spotty access method in the United States, Japan, and parts of Europe. The Internet was accessible everywhere on Earth by the end of 2005. The United States and other nations with significant satellite coverage collaborated to bathe the surface of the planet with the Internet. At the same time the lily pads of WI-FI popped up in place after place until they reached a tipping point and started to multiply geometrically. Wireless phone transmitters approached ubiquity. Abdul's village was so many miles distant from other human habitation that it had a dish of its own to receive a satellite feed into a transmitter that provided hook-up in the village's valley for all the features of the residents' handhelds, including phone, radio, Internet, GPS, and other services. At the table by the kitchen fire in his high mountain home, Abdul surfed in broadband and cast his dynamic nets wherever he chose within the global meshed nets.

Does it seem odd to you that every person in the village received a handheld? Sure, the kids need to get educated and seem without much effort to become whizzes with electronics. But what about Abdul's sixty-year-old grandmother, Bebe? She cannot read and has never traveled farther than a hundred miles from the village. Like a high percentage of grandmas the world over, Abdul's Bebe is conservative in her tribal and religious views. Why waste a handheld on her? She would not know what to do with it. The digital age will revolutionize the young generation but it will be decades before they are running the world.

When Abdul's Bebe received her handheld she was enormously pleased. In the first place, it was a telephone. Until she got her handheld, her use of a phone had been limited to once or twice a month when the family traveled twenty miles to the town in the valley below her village. She would use a pay phone in the town to call her sisters who lived in a small city at the base of the mountain range. During the winter, the family could seldom get through the pass to the lower town so Bebe could make no phone calls at all. Since her handheld streamed video, it was also virtually a television. It would have given her newspapers, too, but they did not mean much to her since she could not read. Bebe's fourteen-year-old granddaughter Ramsia considered her own handheld as the key to her future. Ramsia was not allowed to go to school, which was limited in her valley to boys, but she was determined to get an education. She tutored herself with the reading programs provided by her handheld, sometimes getting some help from Abdul. Ramsia was soon showing off to Bebe, stirring a long dormant determination in the older woman to learn to read. With Ramsia's help Bebe began using the reading and other 3Rs tutorials interfaced with her handheld. Dynamic nets cast from the Hindu Kush village soon flowed about the macro nets at the will of Abdul, Ramsia, and Bebe.

For Abdul Khaled Sr., Bebe's son and the father of Abdul and Ramsia, the handheld quickly became an instrument of independence from the village leader of his tribe. Now that most of the men in his region had the handhelds the devices played an increasing role in their communication and coordination. Information services from various agencies and private companies on the handhelds informed the men of agricultural conditions and marketing matters. Individual interests were fed by the handhelds. Khaled Sr. could follow political news on a Kabul website, forming opinions independent of the tribal chieftain's input. He also enjoyed checking soccer scores and avidly followed the Afghan team in the Asian games. Abdul did too. Father and son often discussed plans to attend the games when Abdul was older.

My Hindu Kush model in this parable is very small scale. There is no scale from small to large for individual humans because each is a separate, sovereign soul and sentient mind. Therefore, to increase the scale of the changes in the lives of the Khaled family what we need to do is to give a handheld to every living human. Does that strike you as impossible? Not only could it happen, but the process is under way. It has become quite conceivable that virtually everyone will soon have a cell phone, and the cell phone is becoming the handheld I have been describing. The development of the mobile Internet is a big movement in technology, software, and content creation. The convergence of all of the features in the handhelds described for the Khaled family is well under way.

A parable about a family named Oko in Nigeria would have the same characters using their handhelds in the same ways. So would one about a Chen family on a farm above the Yellow River in the interior of China. And it would be the same for a Jones family in a project in south Chicago. Any members of any of these actual families could exchange e-mail with counterparts across the world or talk with them on the phone, and while they were talking they could literally be on the same virtual page on the Internet comparing their thoughts or to see each other in real time. In fact, in our parable, Abdul's ChemWhiz netgroup includes in its membership a teenage member of each family, the Okos', the Chens, and the Joneses. Far-fetched? Not at all, as the placement by MIT of its course materials online is showing already. It is included daily in dynamic nets that engage students across the world, as this comment from India describes, "I'm a chemical engineer in India who cannot afford the dream about coming to MIT for further studies, but now I can learn about the state of art in chemical engineering, thanks to MIT."[4] MIT's OpenCourseWare illustrates a future that has arrived for the Indian engineer. It arrived for the families in this parable when they received their handhelds.

As chapter 8 explains, the parable of Abdul can quickly come true. That will probably happen without any central planning. The dimensions of the meshed nets themselves have long since passed the tipping point toward universal hook-up of virtually all the enterprise and knowledge content on Earth. People will come next. Every project small and large toward achieving a handheld for any person is helpful and will accelerate the day when the planet tips into a rapid cascade that will hook up everyone.

TEN USEFUL THINGS TO KNOW ABOUT HOW NETWORKS WILL DIMINISH TERRORISM

We are concerned because relationships are straining and breaking within the human web. Is there a big good thing we can do to terminate the terror threat and heal the human web? If it is true that we do not have to "stoop and build 'em up with worn-out tools," as Rudyard Kipling said, then what tools do we use? Our species has found new tool kits in the past: stone hammers and choppers, metal devices, mechanical inventions, technological devices. As we approach terminating the problem of terrorism, I suggest thinking of the ten useful things we know about networks as fresh instruments in a new tool kit for repairing and retuning the human web. Connecting each person with a handheld device into the meshed nets of communication and content surrounding our species will create a different kind of world, and a better one, than what we now have in which terror thrives.

1. The Structure of a Network Is Not a Hierarchy

A hierarchy relegates people into rows with control coming from the top down. A network puts everyone who is in it on the same page with the control spreading outward from every node. Everyone in the network is heard. The change is from power-down order to networks emerging from complexity. That is a full reversal. The results are large. For example, propaganda from the top down with no means for an upward response except obedience is replaced by freeing individuals to reach into knowledge they share in common for the truth.

The atmosphere of threat and violence that defines terrorism[5] is maintained through regimentation, isolation, and ignorance by tyrants in radical Islam, totalitarian areas of Asia, empires of drug lords, the gang structures of city streets, and elsewhere. Regimentation, isolation, and ignorance thrive in hierarchical structures but cannot survive within networks. The hierarchical form allows movement only up or down, isolating a person in a niche requiring obedience to those above and vesting authority over those below. In the structure of a net, movement begins at a node and is free to go in any direction, with no direction dominant. The fundamental way to prevent further terror is to let individual human beings across the globe think and act for themselves. The opposite idea—control—has a very ugly record. Terror in our times finds roots in rampant tribalism, nationalism, rogue states, cultural loyalties, and religious fervor and factionalism. Underlying them all is dictation to the individual by tyrants who tell people what to think and do. For dictators, the Internet is very bad news. The more people who become nodes in their own right in the human network of the future, the more difficult it will be to seize dictatorial power because that power can only go down—and there is no down direction in the web structure of a net.

Dictatorship is a one-way street for both power and information. Tyranny requires a hierarchy with the tyrant at the top. People ruled by such a structure are told from the top what to think and what to do. They learn to like it that way and never expect to be heard. In ways more gracious than political tyrannies, cultural conditioning easily becomes tyrannical, causing everybody to pretty much think alike, do alike, say little about it, and enjoy it all. I certainly do not think that cultures and traditions are all bad. Their conventions give us stability and coherence. But extreme control in any context is alien to the network of humanity. There are several reasons I can think of—and you may well come up with others—that dictatorship to the individual who is connected to the new, networked world will no longer be effective.

In the 1950s when I majored in political science as an undergraduate at Northwestern University, Professor William H. McGovern was an international intellectual force in the field. In those days you pretty much had to choose between a trendy left and an alarmist right—it was the McCarthy era, after all. McGovern had a lot of prestige as an Asian scholar, and although he was conservative, most students listened to what he said. After 9/11, a college friend of mine mentioned in an e-mail "Do you remember that Professor McGovern warned us that there would be a conflict between East and West?" I did remember. What McGovern had to say in the early 1950s was quite different from the alarm, left and right, about communism that enflamed Joe McCarthy in the early days of the Cold War. Our professor was saying that the nondemocratic heritage of the East—going back long before Islam—would inevitably collide with the individualism born in ancient Athens and carried on in Europe and America. He said that all tyrannies were the same, whether they take the form of oligarchies, aristocracies, theocracies (of any faith), fascism, communism, or just plain autocracies. The point he drove home over and over was that the locus of sovereignty—where the power really is—can come from only one of two places: from the top, like all tyrannies, or from the bottom where it resides in the individual citizen. I now realize that the only way to configure a diagram of the second sort of sovereignty is to sketch a web with every citizen being a node.

A lot of political thinkers and a lot of practical people have gotten very nervous over the idea of every person having real and equal power. That is why Plato's idea of a philosopher king is an easy sell—if only we could find one. Smart people, practical people feel in their gut that it takes some control by a few able folks to make things work. When I was studying these theories fifty years ago, the arguments for individual liberty rested on beliefs in natural rights and Divine endowments. Thomas Jefferson wrote in the American Declaration of Independence: "We hold these Truths to be self-evident, that all Men are created equal, that they are endowed by their Creator with certain unalienable Rights, that among these are Life, Liberty and the Pursuit of Happiness—That to secure these Rights, Governments are instituted among Men, deriving their just Powers from the Consent of the Governed."[6] As Professor McGovern would have pointed out, the power flows up from the governed in the gutsy faith in the citizen that underlies American independence. If the justification for individual freedom and sovereignty is religious and philosophical, why then, would one suppose it works so well? Why does it produce golden ages, record-setting prosperity, and breakthrough creativity? I am convinced it's the nets. We will experience a deep and fundamental change when every person is connected and heard from, because the role in which the handheld places the individual is as a node in that new complexity of nets. The person is no longer a number in a row and rank; the person has been liberated to participate in unlimited dynamic nets. The voice from the top is silenced. The sovereignty is structural because no node is boss; we all are.

The connection between individual sovereignty in a government situation and some network function in that same situation occurred to me as I was reading Steven Strogatz's description of how it could be that a hillside of fireflies synchronize so that they all flash at the same time: "Out of the hubbub, sync somehow emerges spontaneously. Thus we are led to entertain an explanation that seemed unthinkable just a few decades ago—the fireflies organize themselves. No maestro is required, and it doesn't matter what the weather is like. Sync occurs through mutual cuing, in the same way that an orchestra can keep perfect time without a conductor. What is counterintuitive about it is that the insects don't need to be intelligent."[7] As mentioned earlier, Strogatz, who is a founder of the brand-new science of synchronization, also describes how about 10,000 heart cells forming your sinoatrial node set the correct pace for the beats of your heart. "Why do we need so many of these cells, if one can do the job all by itself? Probably because a single leader is not a robust design—a leader can malfunction or die. Instead, evolution has produced a more reliable, democratic system in which thousands of cells collectively set the pace. . . ."[8]

These words may give us the pragmatic key to a future golden age: a single leader is not a robust design—a leader can malfunction or die. Instead, evolution has produced a more reliable, democratic system. Phrasing that differently: do hierarchies work? Network studies are showing us that Nature seldom chooses top-down authority, even when it comes to synchronizing things with as little brain power as a cricket's in love. It turns out that no critter within a food web—another of Nature's common networks—is "in charge" and that the matter of who eats whom emerges from the complexity of the ecology where the web operates. We will wonder in the chapters that follow how much more balanced human affairs can be if we do more networking and less order-giving. If unison of song and light can be achieved by insects, the unison sounds we hear from humanity set free of the strictures of hierarchy should be at least as beautiful and probably infinitely richer.

2. Networks Are the Skeleton of Complexity

We learned in the twentieth century that there can be a great deal to fear from chaos that results from order. It was in many ways the century of totalitarianism in the name of total order. Hitler's invasions and Stalin's purges were conducted to impose order. In his 1949 novel *Nineteen*

Eighty-Four, George Orwell describes the orderly efficiency of the government run by Big Brother:

> They were the homes of the four Ministries between which the entire apparatus of government was divided. The Ministry of Truth, which concerned itself with news, entertainment, education, and the fine arts. The Ministry of Peace, which concerned itself with war. The Ministry of Love, which maintained law and order. And the Ministry of Plenty, which was responsible for economic affairs. Their names, in Newspeak: Minitrue, Minipax, Miniluv, and Miniplenty.[9]

As very much a creature of the twentieth century, until quite recently I would have told you that order and chaos are opposites. I grew up hearing the arguments of Hitler, Stalin, Big Brother, and more friendly order advocates such as the socialists, all justifying their plans as apostles of order for the good of the masses. Order was the skeleton on which government was based. This skeleton of order was necessary to make society not chaotic. Even Churchill saw democracy as a messy if necessary choice. Things got out of hand in tragic ways: protecting and strengthening the structure was so important it was necessary to invade countries and to imprison and execute people who thought otherwise.

How new and wonderful it is to hear that order emerges spontaneously from complexity. We are free to plan beyond a world of imposed order because that sort of world, we have learned the hard way, is the path to chaos. Barabási, who is quoted in the title of this point, tells us: "Networks are only the skeleton of complexity, the highways for the various processes that make our world hum. To describe society we must dress the links of the social network with actual dynamical interactions between people."[10] From that I take a cue to say that the more persons who have handhelds, the more people we hear from, the more this new dynamism can thrive.

Historians ply a trade of teasing out themes from the complexities of human events over time. Sociologists are similarly occupied with identifying trends in human affairs. In the new parlance, these themes and trends could be considered skeletons of human complexities—networks. A long time ago I read something which I think is from Herodotus, the father of history. I have been unable to find it again, but it is a good story to reflect on. It tells of a tribe of people who lived near a desert and became irritated with the south wind because it kept blowing sandstorms across their village. The villagers held a meeting, voted to march against the south wind, set off into the desert to punish it, and were never heard from again. I suppose the mob is often foolish, yet our species has managed to survive so far—overall good sense must have prevailed. I do not think the tyrants get credit for that survival. We have a new insight into why it may be that humanity has not marched off to its own destruction. I think there is great hope for a less violent world, where terror becomes unthinkable, if we look to the emergence of good things from a connected planet. Humanity is not a village that is best dominated by either one dictator or collective foolishness like that against a south wind. We are at our best when we are individually connected in a network that lets us be neither slaves nor a mob. The encouraging robustness of small-world nets is good news in this regard.

3. Sync Emerges from Complexity with Webbed Connections

Alex Lightman, a pioneer of Internet entertainment, knows a lot about the interaction of people and the Internet. He uses the term *4G* to label the "next big thing in computers and communication, and in their convergence."[11] Here he describes a new sort of synchronization that will occur among the nodes (people) within the meshed nets:

> Perhaps government change is the most significant likely impact of 4G, as millions of previously unconnected and uninformed residents wirelessly wise up and team up to make changes that accelerate the virtuous cycle of wireless power plays. . . . Governments will be forced by the most informed and connected pressure groups in history to open up new spectrum and reallocate spectrum for consumer use and unlicensed (and therefore nonmonopolistic) purposes, bringing ever more people into the new political arena.[12]

I do not know at what level, if any, the synchronized pressure of people on government may fit in the new science of spontaneous sync—but the outcomes of both are the same. As Lightman puts it, "informed and connected" sync will exert significant pressures when more people can be heard.

Another sort of sync is captured in the title of Howard Rheingold's book *Smart Mobs*.[13] He uses the term for bunches of teenagers, protesters, and the like keeping in touch through their mobile phones and pagers. The connections allow the mobs to coordinate their actions in powerful new ways. It is well known that the 9/11 hijackers and al Qaeda in general were and are users of cell phones and the Internet. They can act as a sort of smart mob by coordinating through a net of these connections. The alarmists who seem to find something fearsome in each new aspect of the Internet have been quick to say that networking of terrorists indicates a threat from networking itself. The interesting question to me is what will happen when everybody—not just the sinister few—is as well-equipped and skilled at network synchronization as the terrorists were. I do not know the answer to that and am therefore in no position to make a judgment. Looking at the matter from a large perspective, the ranks of terrorism are drawn from individuals who are disconnected from the human web—people of the tatters who are not in sync with society as a whole. I am hopeful that when every person everywhere is connected and can be heard, that will dry up and/or drown out the sources for mischief of the disconnected edges.

More directly to the point of the sort of spontaneous synchronization exhibited by crickets, fireflies, and pacemaker cells, the connection of people throughout the planet to the new digital human nets conjures in my imagination a symphony of harmony that will be global. If you think I am too optimistic, there is something else that is more certain and very positive. When Abdul of our parable is able to read, write, and figure, and is virtually apprenticed as a chemist in Qatar, he will become a very difficult recruit for terrorists. Abdul is in sync with the human web in a productive rhythm.

4. The Structure of a Network Is a Web That Supports Movement in All Directions

Everybody gets connected to everybody; we hear from everybody. In the parable of Abdul, his handheld connected him to what he was learning, to a tutor and mentor, to the test that will qualify him for an apprenticeship and to his future employer. Other family members became nodes in a different set of links, reaching out to information, relatives, business contacts, and political nodes. From the viewpoint of the handheld owners, there is marvelous diversity and freedom in the liberty of linking. As the system matures, each will develop his or her own set of webbed connections, much like the individual e-mail list each of us has that is, in fact, the beginning of our individual meshed nets presence.

From the perspective of the information (content) within the nets the movement in all directions is yet another completely new phenomenon of the digital era. A young person today in developed countries is unfamiliar with global isolation, although many kids still are isolated—in the Hindu Kush, like Abdul before he received his handheld, or in isolated African villages or the Chinese hinterlands, or the remote parts of South America, and elsewhere. For the past 150 years isolation has been lessened by telegraph and telephone, print media improvements, and radio and television. Until media began to shrink the world, scattering of the peoples was common, in primordial, ancient, and recent diasporas. In my own childhood memories, a long-distance phone call was a very big deal and the only real-time media other than radio networks that crossed great distances were short wave radio and cable. I remember hearing Hitler's live voice on the radio: hysterical rapid words of a speech to a huge audience, I was told, set to the background of equally frantic-sounding static that I can still recall. During the years of the war I am sure my parents were unaware of the genocide in Germany against the Jews, although my father was an officer and surgeon in the U.S. Army. Two years after the war was over, my mother showed me some small black-and-white photographs of emaciated bodies stacked in piles. A shudder of horror had gone through the military medical grapevine when a doctor with the liberating troops entering one of the concentration camps had taken pictures and circulated them in the grapevine on his return to the United States. I was eleven when my mother showed me the pictures, telling me she thought I should know.

My experience with the Holocaust pictures is an enlightening one for young people to hear who are used to watching war in real time. But things had actually gotten well connected by the time I saw the pictures in 1947. The newsreels shown at the movies were not all that old. The news from radio and newspapers was real time or only a few hours old.

The doctor had a camera, which had been around for only a century, and had been reasonably portable for a much shorter time. He had crossed the Atlantic to get to the camp and crossed back to deliver the images to the other side of the world. People had been crossing the Atlantic for nearly 500 years. Nine centuries earlier than the great Age of Exploration when Da Gama, Columbus, and Magellan opened the oceans as global highways, information was isolated and remote. In the early seventh century when Prophet Muhammad founded Islam, his knowledge of other faiths came by caravan across the deserts of Arabia. Princeton Near Eastern Studies Professor Emeritus Bernard Lewis describes the flavor of religious materials available in Mecca in the early 600s when Muhammad was a young man:

> Modern scholars have inferred, from Muslim versions of Bible stories, that the early Muslims' biblical knowledge was indirectly acquired, probably from Jewish and Christian traders and travelers whose information was affected by midrashic and apocryphal influences. The tradition speaks of certain people called Hanifs, pagan Meccans who were dissatisfied with the prevailing idolatry of their people and sought a purer form of religion, but yet were unwilling to accept either Judaism or Christianity. It might well be among them that Muhammad's spiritual origins are to be sought.[14]

It is folly to speculate whether the attacks of 9/11 happened because the wrong information about the contents of the Bible rode a camel into ancient Mecca. It is crucial to realize the enormous contrast to a seventh-century camel ride that we already experience in spreading information in every direction through the Internet to every person connected so far. A key value to be obtained from making every person on the planet a node in the meshed nets is that the isolation of information will end completely. From new things we are learning about how nets work, we can expect that the apocryphal versions of ideas are less likely to travel far, as we will see below. Context and the law of the few bolster the truth to prominence.

The most basic change that worldwide distribution of the handhelds will cause is to flood the planet with ideas and actions that emerge from the complexity of human habitation. This is the reverse of the age-old picture of the tribal chief directing the activities of his underlings.

Mechanisms of downward control are replaced by the validity of connections within a dynamic net to fulfill its purpose. Those links go freely in all directions, and rightfully should connect to all persons.

5. Nets Clarify Relationships and Let Us Experience Context

Nets, as opposed to top-down organizations, arrange their nodes into context. Why is this node linked to that node? The answer is that they are drawn to each other by meaning. In the parable of Abdul, Bebe links to her sisters, and Khaled Sr. links to his business partners. Bebe casts a net of family relationships, and her son casts one where the nodes each have a role in the business he is transacting. Al Qaeda also has a network, whose chatter is the source of warning on which the decision is made to raise or lower terror alerts. Fascism spawned its evil from the orders of a single top leader who sent orders down a military tree structure. Today's terrorism is a context from which one node can wreak horror as a suicide bomber of a tiny web cell can carry out an attack independent of other cells. It would seem that the terrorists are showing us the efficiency of acting in context—and it is frightening when they do it. Its effectiveness should, I think, not discourage us from connecting everybody, but rather do the opposite. Seeing to it that all persons participate in the human web is a lot safer than leaving it to the bad guys.

Informational content within the web of a network links together in the same way that people do. A node about an earthquake in Algeria quickly becomes linked to other nodes about earthquakes and about Algeria, creating a weblet to surf to learn about the event and related ideas that are its context. This characteristic of networks is discussed in detail in chapter 6. It is a major deterrent to terrorism to the extent that truth is a deterrent. Hitler bragged about telling a "Big Lie" until people believed it. That should be a lot harder to do when everybody everywhere can check out what they hear and find it in context.

6. A Common Type of Network Form Is into Small Worlds

The most basic principle of network theory in the venue of political affairs is that the human web is a small-world network. It was noticed as such by Stanley Milgram's project that revealed what has become known as the six degrees of separation of individual people from each other. In his book *Linked*, Professor Barabási uses the travels of Saint Paul, calling him a master of the network, to illustrate the impact of a small worlds on the spread of Christianity:

> The message had to be spread. So he used his firsthand knowledge of the social network of the first century's civilized world from Rome to Jerusalem to reach and convert as many people as he could. He walked nearly 10,000 miles in the next twelve years of his life. He did not wander randomly, however, he reached out to the biggest communities of his era, to the people and places where the faith could generate most effectively. He was the first and by far the most effective salesperson of Christianity, using theology and social networks equally effectively. . . . Paul . . . became a bridge builder between early Christian communities.[15]

The small-world network does not look anything like the evenly spaced knots and strings of the fishnets used by Jesus' apostles. It looks like the pattern of Paul's conversions. There are big clusters, key hubs with connectors that put the more dense nodes in touch with other communities of dense nodes. That is the same pattern that a projection of the interconnections within the nodes of the Internet reveals. For decades networks studied by the mathematicians (*graphs*, in their parlance) were assumed to be regular—something like fishnets—or random, with no pattern at all. As Strogatz relates the story, "By 1996, the twin fictions of regular and random networks were starting to look less and less plausible every day. Anyone surfing the Web could sense it was both a pattern and a maze, where Web pages link mainly to others on the same topic but occasionally veer off onto idiosyncratic byways."[16] Strogatz and Watts then turned to explaining what was going on and they found and described what have come to be called small-world networks. They, and soon others, began discovering small worlds in many, many places.

I predict that when every person in the physical human web (everyone alive) is also a node in the virtual web of meshed nets (they all have handhelds and everyone can hear them) small-world network theory will become the basis of theoretical political science and sociology.

Those of us who still hold the truths to be self-evident that we are each endowed by our Creator with certain unalienable rights will simply say "We told you so. Power resides in the individual." The pragmatists will be happy, too, because they will have demonstrable proof.

The question then becomes how terrorism fares in a population that forms a small-world network. Perhaps the terror groups are hubs that can be isolated and destroyed as the technical people are learning to do on the Internet. There will be other things to be learned and done by examining human relations as a small-world network. You may have already thought of some. One very big one is the law of few that is the following point.

7. Scale-Free Net Structure Elevates Winners in a Small-World Network

When I was studying political science at Northwestern, communism was still widely respected. Many who thought it was a good idea were upset and disappointed at Stalin and his cronies for taking what they saw as a beautiful idea and using it to engineer their totalitarian takeover and control. I suppose even we of the conservative bent thought Marx had a good idea. We just did not think it would work. The ideal touted in my college years was: from each according to our ability to each according to his need. It was a Robin Hood gallantry of robbing the rich to feed the poor. That does not happen in a small-world network: the rich get richer. Could it be that because the human species is inherently a small-world network schemes of equality will never work?

Barabási's group at Notre Dame University did the seminal work on the power law aspects of scale-free networks. The network of ideas and terms surrounding this subject include the law of the few, the fact that the rich get richer, and the 80/20 law. Here is how Barabási describes some of the real world manifestations of these rules. He starts with an observation of Italian economist Vilfredo Pareto:

> An avid gardener, he noticed that 80 percent of his peas were produced by only 20 percent of the peapods. A careful observer of economic inequalities, he saw that 80 percent of Italy's land was owned by only 20 percent of the population. More recently, Pareto's Law or Principle, known

> as the 80/20 rule, has been turned into the Murphy's Law of management: 80 percent of profits are produced by only 20 percent of the employees, 80 percent of customer problems are created by only 20 percent of consumers, 80 percent of decisions are made during 20 percent of meeting time, and so on.[17]

So much for the ideal of from each according to ability to each according to need! Some peapods do all the work! That is not all bad for the pods that do less yet receive the nourishment they need from the common vine. Perhaps the political reality is similar within the human web, which is a small-world where we are separated by the famed six degrees: 20 percent keep things working well. Clearly the 20 percent of Pareto's peapods were the most capable in the garden. We can expect that in a fully connected world as well. Looking at it as the optimist I am, I expect the best 20 percent to take the lead in governing, sciences, and social areas. If that seems to you totally cockeyed, I think you will give me this: almost any 20 percent group is better than one Hitler or Saddam Hussein in charge of things.

There is another advantage in the law of the few that is covered in chapter 6, which deals with the absorption of what is known by humankind to be studied and learned there. The few best and most important topics and sources move to become the top 20 percent of the virtual resources, which are then studied in common by everyone. This common knowledge puts every person who has a handheld on the same page as everyone else in studying a subject. That alone should build enough worldwide understanding to diminish terrorism considerably.

8. Structural Nets and Functional Nets Are Not the Same

This topic is for visionaries, because we can only see hints of what will happen when the functional nets encompass everyone on the planet. All the billions upon billions of connections among the URLs and those that link the content of Web pages compose the structural phase of the digital meshed nets. All the human activity within that connectivity is the function phase: it is what people are doing. If the day can come when every individual is connected to the structural nets, the functional nets will be the environment for massive commerce, communication, and exchange. At the level of the health and function of the human web, John Stuart Mill has this advice, written in 1859 in *On Liberty*:

> If all mankind minus one, were of one opinion, and only one person were of the contrary opinion, mankind would be no more justified in silencing that one person, than he, if he had the power, would be justified in silencing mankind. Were an opinion a personal possession of no value except to the owner; if to be obstructed in the enjoyment of it were simply a private injury, it would make some difference whether the injury was inflicted only on a few persons or on many. But the peculiar evil of silencing the expression of an opinion is, that it is robbing the human race; posterity as well as the existing generation; those who dissent from the opinion, still more than those who hold it. If the opinion is right, they are deprived of the opportunity of exchanging error for truth: if wrong, they lose what is almost as great a benefit, the clearer perception and livelier impression of truth, produced by its collision with error.[18]

Nothing will be more interesting to watch in the functional aspects of the future age of universal connection than the valuing and impact of individual expression. The answer so far to billions now asking, "Can you hear me yet?" is "No." We are still minus a lot more than one opinion from mankind.

9. The Net Medium Richly Interfaces Gestalts and Isomorphs

I have not thought of ways this point relates to the elimination of terror. Perhaps you will. It is the central point of chapter 5.

10. Epidemics Cascade across Nets

You paint a very optimistic picture of the wonderful things caused by networks, you may be thinking, but who is in charge? My answer is simple: the lack of human control is why the changes are taking place. What the content of a net does is at least in part determined by the structure of the net in which it is contained. One thing it does very well is to cascade when it reaches a tipping point.

The emergence of the United States of America from the British colonies in the eighteenth century is fine case study for a supreme human accomplishment achieved with no one in charge. Am I saying management is meaningless? No, George Washington and the money guys stepped in to direct some events and processes as the American colonies declared and won their independence from England. Management was not in place to define the goals, set the agenda, or cause the support. Just as the Internet has done in our lifetime, the American Revolution grew from the bottom up, forming a network that released an unexpected flood of creativity and accomplishment.

The fellow who caused the American Revolution to tip into war was hardly in charge of anything. He probably did not even fire the shot that was heard around the world. Captain John Parker ordered the line of seventy minutemen he had summoned to the Lexington Green to hold their positions as seven hundred British Red Coats advanced. No one knows who fired the first shot, but it was what tipped America from tyranny into liberty. Captain Parker's statue still guards the bridge at Concord where the fighting continued on that pivotal April 19, 1775, until the British began a retreat toward Lexington and then Boston. The emergence of the patriot force was not planned and not managed. A motley force of 15,000 armed men from across New England responded to the Alarm of April 19, as the phase transition had been set off from English subject to American patriot. Many of these individuals did not know each other and became linked into a new entity that did not seek them out but which spread like a web in a nonhierarchical pattern. It was a web—or network—of desire for independence.

One Fourth of July, in the spirit of the day, I was poking around in some of my family's records and discovered that two of my ancestors, Timothy Eastman and Chileab Merrick, answered the Alarm of April 19. Page 160 of the Massachusetts Revolution Rolls reads: "Timothy Eastman of Hadley enlisted as a private in Capt. Eliakim Smith's company, later commanded by Capt. Moses Kellog, which marched 4/20/1775 in response to the alarm of 4/19/1775; returned home . . . service of 9 days."[19] From my family records I know that Timothy was 39 years old and was living with his wife, Anna, in Hadley, Massachusetts. Their firstborn, a daughter, had died two years before, and Anna was pregnant with their next child who was born the following fall. Chileab, age 28, lived a few miles away in Wilbraham, Massachusetts. When he marched toward the business on the road to Boston he left his wife, Abigail, and a baby daughter at home. Forty-three of the minutemen were killed in the events following the tipping point on Lexington Green. Eastman and Merrick survived, and I carry their genes passed along by children born to them after their service in the Revolution.

The epidemic of patriotism that swept America into war for independence spread through a network of communication mounted on horseback or moving on foot. Sam Adams and Paul Revere did a good job of sparking its dynamics, energizing a web, and not giving orders. It is astounding to know that every person on Earth could and probably soon will have a device in his or her hand through which a motivational epidemic can cascade. It seems to me that will be a sweeping deterrent to terrorism. For one thing, with everyone connected it will be much harder to isolate and indoctrinate the foot soldiers of terror. The devices will also be balanced as sources of information and education as well as communication. Access to the truth is anathema to terror.

DYNAMIC NETS GIVE US INTERACTIVITY AND MORE THAN JUST ACCESS

It should be emphasized again that we need to break the bad habit of thinking of the Internet as just access—as a substitute for reading a newspaper or going to the library. A brand-new, virtual, dynamic world is upon us. Things are morphing into a new tomorrow because of the dynamic interchange of two vast and enormously complex macro networks that have never existed before. The first is the structural net—an interactive tangle of networks converging communications, media, the Internet, untold numbers of servers and hard drives full of webbed information, stuff going to and from satellites, and many other networks and netlets. This massive mesh is getting close to becoming the one, seamless network it will be the day after tomorrow. The structural net already contains significant content that is pivotal to business, learning, and other major aspects of human affairs—and more pours into it every day. We experience this macro structural network every time we go online or use our cell phone.

The second macro network, the human functional one, is not nearly as finished as the first, and that is something we should be taking care of with determination and haste. When it is complete, this comprehensive functional net will consist of each person on Earth as an active node, with every node connected to every other node and linked interactively into the previously described structural net.

The variety of possible dynamic nets incorporating relations between the two macro networks is limited only by one's imagination. There is no limit to the combinations that could be made among people and the content of the macro net of information. Will the dynamic nature of the nets serve the purposes of the terrorists? I think the contrary is true. Power is hard to pin down in a network, and dictatorial control is difficult without a structural platform. The human web that has evolved over the eons will have a virtual mirror in the connectivity of all within the digital meshed nets. Will making that complete and whole help to heal and preserve us against the tattering of terror? I hope so, and I think so.

NOTES

1. J. R. McNeill and William H. McNeill, *The Human Web: A Bird's-eye View of World History* (New York: W.W. Norton, 2003), book jacket.
2. Rudyard Kipling, *If*, www.swarthmore.edu/~apreset1/docs/if.html [accessed 21 May 2003].
3. Steven Strogatz, *Sync: The Emerging Science of Spontaneous Order* (New York: Hyperion, 2003), 13–14.
4. MIT OpenCourseWare, additional quotes, ocw.mit.edu/global/additional quotes.html [accessed 9 April 2003].
5. *Webster's Unabridged Dictionary*, Unabridged.merriam-webster.com/cgi-bin/unabridged?va=terrorism [accessed 6 April 2003].
6. Thomas Jefferson, *The American Declaration of Independence*, 1776.
7. Strogatz, *Sync*, 13.
8. Strogatz, *Sync*, 15.
9. George Orwell, *Big Brother*, www.online-literature.com/orwell/1984/1/ [accessed 22 May 2003].
10. Albert-László Barabási, *Linked* (Cambridge, Mass.: Perseus), 225.
11. Alex Lightman with William Rojas, *Brave New Unwired World: The*

Digital Big Bang and the Infinite Internet (New York: John Wiley & Sons, 2002), ix.

12. Lightman, *Brave New Unwired World,* 9.

13. Howard Rheingold, *Smart Mobs* (Cambridge, Mass.,: Perseus, 2002).

14. Bernard Lewis, *The Arabs in History* (Oxford: Oxford University Press, 1993), 35.

15. Barabási, *Linked,* 4.

16. Strogatz, *Sync,* 238.

17. Barabási, *Linked,* 66.

18. John Stuart Mill, *On Liberty,* 1859, www.serendipity.li/jsmill/on_lib.html [accessed 23 May 2003].

19. M. Emily Eastman, *History and Genealogy of Deacon Joseph Eastman of Hadley, Mass.* (Westfield, Mass.: M. Emily Eastman), 26.

4

MALL NETS: E-COMMERCE HAS SHOWN THE WAY

> While economic conditions have only recently showed signs of improving, technology has never stopped. Today's wireless data networks have larger footprints, are more reliable, and feature greater throughput than their predecessors. Mobile devices have become ubiquitous—far more powerful, less expensive, and suitable for data-driven applications.
>
> —Mobile Marketing[1]

This excerpt from a mobile marketing white paper dated April 2003 captures the happy hype of the industry in its youth. There is good reason for the happiness. The mobile marketers are repeating the upward spiral that wired online commerce began in the mid-1990s, leading to the current time when doing business on the Internet is established, proven, and successful. Although e-commerce is destined to grow greatly in the future, its many successes so far are certain. The comments of a man who hyped online business in its early years were reported in an article titled "Requiem for a Cheerleader: Silicon Alley Magazine Is Dead."[2] The story appeared October 8, 2001. It quoted the deceased magazine's publisher Jason McCabe Calacanis, who said, "The story is over, you can't have a magazine about unemployed people. You can't have a magazine about people who are taking time off." Calacanis's insight in another comment in the story is key: "Having a magazine about the Internet now is like having a magazine about refrigerators. What can you say about them? They work."

If you have never done business on the Internet, you have been walking right by the huge and humming refrigerator full of business being done online. One day soon, mobile commerce may get you involved without your ever having peeked into the wired enterprise colossus. When you begin doing mobile business, you will be using dynamic nets whose links include establishment online enterprises (the refrigerator), but you will be doing it in your hand with a device that has far more features than your desktop computer. Your handheld will not only contain the virtual malls you browse. It will also be your shopping list, your sales clerk, your credit card, and your receipt. When you shop in a brick-and-mortar mall, your handheld will be your driver's license, parking ticket, and car keys, your map of the mall with a marker to show you at all times where you are, your shopping list with a record of past purchases, your budget, your credit card, and other things yet to be thought up. The financial and inventory aspects of your transactions at a virtual or physical mall will take place within the meshed nets, independent of the device in your hand or your desktop's hard drive at home.

The subject of transforming commercial enterprise into meshed nets is enormous and multifaceted. This chapter approaches it in only three ways. First, there is my prediction that search engines will and must morph into software that produces nets before they will be really effective in the future meshed nets setting of massive mobile commerce—or any other online purposes. Second, and corollary to the first idea, I believe that the platform of e-commerce stores—or really any website—must change from lists to webs to harness the network medium meaningfully. Third are some thoughts about how the ten useful things to know about networks described in other chapters would apply to commerce when handhelds have been distributed to everybody around the globe.

Each of these three perspectives is critically important to education, although they are approached here in a broad and general view. As I have stated earlier, it seems instructive to me to approach education with an understanding of the larger world, as opposed to trying to conform a vision of the larger world to a set view of education. Educators attempt to force that conformity by using search engines to find material to be extracted from the Internet and placed in student resources where the Internet is cut off by a firewall, in effect replicating a printed study page. A real-world approach would be to work within the Internet to connect study materials to a cognitive web for students to enter to learn a subject. Being able to do that well involves the points discussed in this chapter.

NET-MAKERS—BEYOND SEARCH ENGINES

In March 2003 I attended a national conference of librarians. One full afternoon of the program was devoted entirely to Google, and it drew several hundred attenders. The description of one of the sessions raised this question: "Should academic or corporate users use the resources of the research library or simply type queries into Google? There are good reasons to believe that libraries offer more, but statistics suggest that users are increasingly choosing Google."[3] The way things are today, that question is not limited to looking up things for which we used to count on librarians. The day I am writing this, two stacks of brand-new yellow pages books are sitting on my curbside waiting for the recycle truck to cart them away. The stack of the free directories rejected by apartment dwellers in my building has gotten higher in recent years as more and more of them have acquired computers and cell phones. Looking things up in the digital milieu is becoming the preferred method of finding more and more things, and Google is currently dominating that process on the Internet.

Google is commonly thought of as a search engine, but is that what Google is? I do not think so. It is a hybrid text search and net-maker. The big improvement in finding things on the Internet and elsewhere in digital realms will come when the text search is only a tool for net-making. I remember when a text search of the Internet really did bring up a list on your computer screen of nearly every appearance among millions of web pages of the string of text you had entered. I can date my memory of that to early 1997 when I started working at an Internet company. As I led an online research team over the four ensuing years, I watched day by day as the pure text search became more and more useless, drowning in the sheer volume of new web pages, becoming irrelevant to the increasing number of dynamic pages and being grabbed on to by the managers of the search sites to turn searches into lucrative revenue streams attracted by weighted tags. When products could buy placement in search engines, that business lost its innocence.

Google came along as a phenomenon unto itself. After the first time I used it I never went back to any other so-called search engine. It has been explained to me that the links Google puts at the top in the return for a topic searched are the ones that are receiving the most hits for that topic within the Internet. I know the formula is not that simple, but that is the general idea. The vaunted team that runs Google has become a legend among the Internet initiated. As the librarians pointed out in the description for the conference, the majority of people prefer Google to librarians. Other sessions at the library conference focused on how the librarians, too, use and love Google. My guess is that the reason Google works so well is that it largely operates on network principles. It manages to link your node of interest to a matching node of information that offers a nugget itself and links out to other ideas in context. Although there is undoubtedly text-word searching going on in preparing a Google reply to a query, there is much more. I assume Google is operating on some version of the 80/20 rule: Google would only consider 20 percent of the raw response. That 20 percent would be the links that are most often visited, following the network behavior of the rich getting richer. Context is playing a role when Google evaluates what sort of other Web pages are linking to one under consideration for selection. The idea of scale-free is probably in there somewhere, eliminating any sort of proscribed curve and allowing for a few links to rise disproportionately to the top and the rest to have little relevance.

Whether my guesses are right or off the mark, one thing is clear. Google is avoiding the awful bore of just listing web pages in the order in which the text in a search appears the most precisely and often. I hope the effect of the efficacy of what Google and similar search services are doing will lead to a major change in how we know what is out there in cyberspace. The web pages need ways to tell the search services more about themselves than what words they contain. They need to brag about their connections. Of course we have come full circle. Google picks sites by evaluating what it is connected to, and the other sites that connect to it have made judgments, by checking out what a site has to say, and have affirmed that site by linking to it.

I seldom use Google with the goal of expecting a link I need to appear at the top, although that does happen with amazing frequency. I view Google instead as giving me an entry point into a preexisting weblet of what I am looking for. I think I realized that what I look for on the Internet is not a link but a weblet on the day I read Billy Barty's obituary in the *New York Times* in December 2000. Barty, who was 70 years-old when he died, was 3 feet 9 inches tall. I would have called him a dwarf until I visited his website, which is still online at billybarty.com. When I read the obituary I did not know much about little people except from family stories about one I had heard from my mother. Her grandmother was the aunt of a circus midget named Major Mite who was famous in the early twentieth century. The midget was a first cousin of my grandfather, whom he visited whenever the circus was in town, and my mother remembered him well. The Barty obituary mentioned that he had a website and I decided to take a look. The first thing I learned was not to use the words *dwarf* or *midget,* because the preference of those whom the words label is *little person* and they do not like the other two words. Within ten minutes after I arrived at the website, I knew a lot about little people. The Barty site is a rich web of information. It links out to descriptions of causes of the shortness of stature, for which there is a web of medical, health, and genetic information. Another set of nodes describes and has places to order clothing that properly fits a little person. Another path leads to the nodes of little people organizations, which link in many directions to information and activities. There are wonderful stories of Billy Barty's acting prowess and charity, along with several moving tributes posted in his memory. He must have been a truly great guy and the interconnections at billybarty.com of many aspects of his life gave me a rich understanding of him and little people in general.

No one link served up by a search engine effectively delivers the complexity offered by the Internet. Instead, a service like Google helps you connect to some meaningful skeleton within the enormous complexity of what is out there in cyberspace. Any one of the nodes I mentioned on the Barty website can belong in many different skeletons. It takes the idea of the little person Billy Barty to cause the exact configuration that we call his website. Each organization of little people linked to the Barty site is a unique skeleton of connections. Any of many movies in which Barty appeared as an actor would form a web configured by the relationships among other actors, the director, the story, the setting, and so on. Barty appeared, for example, in *The Bride of Frankenstein,* which would appear as a node in a collection of movies about Frankenstein. The purpose of what we call search engines is to put a searcher in touch with a node within a web that connects to the networked information she seeks.

The connections among web pages are probably at least as important to consider in locating useful websites as the content of the pages. It is my predication and hope that connections among pages will become increasingly coherent and useful so that great topical networks are skeletons that rise from the chaos of the billions of pages in the enormous Internet soup, where little skeletons like your personal interactive resume are just as useful to you as the giants are to the public. While the process of linking and cleansing and relinking is continuing to form global Internet content, the human web is becoming digitized, too. When we all have a handheld, we humans will form a global net of connected individuals. An example of what that will mean is discussed in chapter 1 where the network of birders who share the sighting by one of their members (nodes) can quickly be shared to all members (nodes). What we still continue to call search engines will become net-makers that offer webs of pertinent nodes as entry points for the searcher into interconnected nets of relevant material. The first page of a Google response to a search is very often very close to that description: a web (although it is still interfaced like a list) of pertinent nodes from which to choose an entry point for the subject that was entered into the Google search box. The transformation from text searching to net-making is fundamental to the big breakthrough for e-business, as the next section explains.

THE MOTHER OF ALL MALLS

Although some aspects of e-commerce run with the efficiency of a refrigerator, the potential probably has been barely tapped so far. An indicator that great changes can be made is that a lot of the established e-commerce websites are not yet interfaced along network principles. It is safe to say that the ones that function as nets have succeeded, often spectacularly. Two of the purest net-based websites are Amazon.com and eBay.com. Amazon links its products in an amazing number of ways. When you look for something, Amazon always comes right back with a web to surf. If you ask for a certain book or author, that book or author appears as the main node on a page that also offers you nodes for the author, similar authors, other books by the person who wrote the book you requested, and a group of books other people chose who bought the book you requested. There is also a node with reviews and often one with some pages from the central book. In a moment, your eye can grasp all of these nodes. These choices are graphically unique with different fonts and colors—there is no strong sense of vertical lists to go down. The marketplace site eBay is an amazingly complex collection of links to products and people, with descriptions for each and many ways to connect that and this to this and that. A seller or buyer links among particular nodes within the chaos to form a dynamic network that becomes his transaction. Meshed into all of that is the interlinking of thousands of sellers and buyers whose nodes link to products that interest them individually.

The dazzling connectivity of Amazon and eBay are in contrast to the dreary way most catalogs are arranged in websites. The catalogs tend to mirror the hierarchical databases in which the items that are for sale are archived. There is a web page for the cameras, another page for the tripods, and another page for the flash units because in the photographic company's files there is separate database page for each. Merchants also think of a store as having a display case for the cameras, the tripods over against the wall and the flash units on a shelf behind the counter. In the brick-and-mortar store, the salesperson physically brings together camera, tripod, and flash so the customer can evaluate them as a whole. Web pages that mirror databases are often clumsy at mixing and matching. That takes a lot of the effectiveness and fun out of shopping online. Amazon and eBay have shown that there is a better way.

The advance of broadband is releasing new creativity that can energize e-business and is likely to significantly increase consumer participation and sales. A report urging retailers to use broadband to give their online presence a facelift makes these suggestions: "Retailers must also develop more advanced product-centric tools: Electronics and toy retailers need to implement Amazon-esque customer ratings systems; store-based apparel retailers must catch up to catalogs that offer dynamic zoom and pan; and music and video retailers should beef up streaming media libraries to all consumers to sample before buying."[4]

Macromedia, the makers of important web software applications including Director, Dreamweaver, and Flash are marketing what they call rich media. It introduces a method that steps correctly into the future by strongly applying networking to interfacing a website. The idea is that the individual items to be interfaced remain cataloged in their database—hierarchical pigeonholes—but are pulled out and displayed dynamically in Flash pages that are freed from hierarchy or any other structural formula. The function of the page determines how its parts are displayed, and that function can be ordered up and modified interactively by the virtual visitor. I love big red shirts. In the rich media world, if the mood struck me to shop for one, I could go to a page on the Internet and tell it I wanted to compare all the big red shirts the page could find. I could ask the page to display the shirts first by the fabric they were made of. I could tell it not to display any shirt I would have to dry clean or iron. When I got down to the few shirts I liked best, I would zoom in on buttons, compare pockets, and then arrange my favorites by price to make a final pick. Three or four clicks more should have the shirt on the way to me for delivery in a day or two.

There are two main differences between the red shirt experience I just described and what it would be like to visit a brick-and-mortar mall to shop. First, at the mall, I could try the shirt on. There are already merchants online who will let you provide your measurements so you can see what a shirt would look like on a virtual you. These will surely get better and better until they will be just about as good as looking in the mirror. You will not be able to sense the feel or temperature—yet. The other difference is that in the brick-and-mortar mall experience you are limited to the red shirts that happen to be available at stores in the mall that carry shirts. A networked online shopper in a year or two should be able to virtually gather up every red shirt in every store on the planet to admire and compare so she can buy the one that is the best in the world for her. The mobile device held in her hand will be the mother of all malls. It will not only make her mobile as she shops, from home, office, on the road, or anywhere she is—it also mobilizes the red shirts and every other item of commerce.

TEN USEFUL THINGS TO KNOW ABOUT NETWORKS AND BUSINESS

1. The Structure of a Network Is Not a Hierarchy

The subject of this chapter is the business arena, where networks forced their own entry when given the opportunity. The meshed nets are the biggest such opportunity in all of history. For business, once the Internet tipped and began expanding toward epidemic proportions, nothing could impede the relocation of commerce into its networks. The reason is obvious: commerce is a matter of interchange, of networking. It does not take an expert to see that commerce forms a web. Commerce is exchange, it is about what goes where. It is an interplay of webs of supply and demand, inventory and delivery, sell and buy. The single up/down directionalism and tree structure of a hierarchy bring commerce to a halt.

2. Networks Are the Skeleton of Complexity

John Holland begins his classic-in-its-own-time book on complexity, *Hidden Order*, with this description of the wonders of real commerce:

> On an ordinary day in New York City, Eleanor Petersson goes to her favorite specialty store to pick up a jar of pickled herring. She fully expects the herring to be there. Indeed, New Yorkers of all kinds consume vast stocks of food of all kinds, with hardly a worry about continued supply. This is not just some New Yorker persuasion; inhabitants of Paris and Delhi and Shanghai and Tokyo expect the same. It's a sort of magic that everywhere is taken for granted. Yet these cities have no central planning commissions that solve the problems of purchasing and distributing supplies. Nor do they maintain large reserves to buffer fluctuations; their food would last less than a week or two if the daily arrivals were cut off.[5]

Within the teeming, churning dynamic web of commerce in a city and across the globe, Eleanor Petersson completes a pickled herring transaction. She can also do this on the Internet with a greater selection of herring and prices, delivery to her door, and other added perks. If the store where she gets the herring is a distance from her home, her online purchase may save her time. Eleanor also has the new convenience of not having to ship pickled herring to her sister who moved from New York to Montana when she got married because the e-commerce merchant that sells herring will ship it directly to her sister's new home in Butte. The herring transactions—either on the ground if Eleanor physically goes to the specialty store, or within the Internet if the herring is ordered online—are brief dynamic skeletons of order that form within the complexity of commerce. They are certainly a part of the magic that makes commerce work with no one in charge. When they occur in the meshed nets, instead of being trudged out by foot on the ground, they often offer a richer transaction experience. This increased richness will become much greater in the future.

3. Sync Emerges from Complexity with Webbed Connections

When each person on Earth has a handheld device which he or she is using to interact with everything that is for sale anywhere and with every other buyer and seller around the globe, whatever forces are inherent that cause sync will be released in a very big way. Point 10 below concerns what is known so far about how synchronization acts in releasing fads that multiply sales. But we can doubt that fads are the whole story. The world economy today is a synthesis that includes many markets and consumer groups that are isolated from one another. Universal individual access to all enterprise means everybody is going to shop in one big virtual mall. Will this remain commercial chaos or, as was true for Eleanor in the illustration above, can she count on the pickled herring being on the virtual shelf when she goes shopping? The answer to that is unknowable at this time, but we do know that sync can cause self-organized states as a couple of studies of automobile traffic have shown. Strogatz describes what that was like in one of the studies: "At a critical density of traffic—about 35 vehicles in each lane per mile of road—all the cars and trucks spontaneously synchronized, traveling down the highway like a solid block."[6] I predict that sync will show up in interesting new ways as the arena of enterprise consolidates into one mammoth, global, virtual mall.

4. The Structure of a Network Is a Web That Supports Movement in All Directions

As the earlier Amazon.com and eBay.com examples illustrate, e-commerce that maximizes linking in multidirections has prospered. Another aspect of the commercial world that has migrated into the digital nets in a very big way is employment. For enterprises seeking employees to connect with people seeking jobs, and vice versa, the digital networks are far more efficient and comprehensive than methods in the old days of snail mail and print ads. Mailing letters to addresses from want ads is a series of single target contacts. A digital search has the effect to sending a current in dozens of directions through a dense web of wires, glass, and beams.

5. Nets Clarify Relationships and Let Us Experience Context

Each step in the red shirt illustration discussed earlier was a placing of the shirts into a new and different context. When I shop for shirts at a clothing store, I will find any one shirt in just one context. A red shirt would probably be hanging in a rack of shirts of every color in stock, grouped by size. Perhaps a second red shirt identical to the one hanging in the rack would be displayed on a mannequin nearby or in the store window, but that would be about it for context. As I am shopping in a store, I can take the shirt to the skirt department and see how it would look with a skirt I am interested in buying, but I would probably not be allowed to carry it out of the store and into a competitive shop to see how it looked with a skirt over there.

In the virtual shopping world, moving things around in context is a natural outgrowth of being able to change how things are linked to each other. Painting museums often have a way for you to put a group of images together on a web page so you can see them all at once and learn about them from comparisons. I think we will see a lot more of that kind of selectivity and context-building in e-commerce websites very soon. Broadband will help by speeding up the arrival of web pages and rich media that dynamically pulls products to a page is, in effect, context creation. When you are considering buying your favorite kind of shirt, you will be able to group it with any other item in the net malls to consider it in the context of color, style, texture, or other factors. You will be able to shift and alter the context of your decision by changing and grouping components to your whim.

6. A Common Type of Network Form Is into Small Worlds

Economic theorists of the future will provide a framework for understanding the economics of the new globally networked enterprise system that is now forming. For now we know that e-commerce has developed within the Internet and that the Internet is a small-world network. It will be fascinating to watch and explain what form enterprises, large and small, take in this environment. Will there be a few great clusters? Will there be hubs through which most business travels? Who will be the connectors? I will not venture to guess here, but will say that it seems certain that the global economy is already undergoing structural change resulting from the growing importance of the meshed nets. That seems like a good idea to me.

7. Scale-Free Net Structure Elevates Winners in a Small-World Network

How will the 80/20 rule and the rich-get-richer trend of the scale-free networks affect e-commerce when everyone has a handheld? If the macro interconnects of e-commerce—the global net mall—turns out to be a small-world network, that means it will be scale-free. Perhaps that will mean 20 percent of companies have most of the business and the other 80 percent all have just a little bit of business. From my understanding, the power law underlying scale-free networks does not predict monopolies—perhaps some extremely large companies but not just one big one. The 80/20 ratio precludes communism where all are equal, but if it also precludes monopoly, that would be a good thing. I would be comfortable with 20 percent dominant so long as the rest of us can still make our own living and run small enterprises if we so choose. As we saw in the last chapter, Pareto's peapods get along that way. Perhaps that is just how things are.

8. Structural Nets and Functional Nets Are Not the Same

It is a functional, not a structural, net that keeps the herring on the store shelf in John Holland's description of the stocking of food in cities. The digital age is getting very good at tracking some of the functions. These days there are computers that follow the progress of a crate on a ship at sea knowing it contains a part that will be soldered into a memory board at a specific factory on a certain date in the future. There are bar codes on shipments that tell computers tracking the packages where they are and when they reach their destinations. The structural platform of cables, wires, etched chips, and signal-laden beams are merely the structure where the information travels. Network theory helps us understand a fundamental difference. Barabási tells us that "we must move beyond structure and topology and start focusing on the dynamics that take place along the links."[7] The mother of all malls is not a place. It is a macro dynamic mesh of commerce webs into which we all will soon cast our own dynamic nets to do our shopping.

9. The Net Medium Richly Interfaces Gestalts and Isomorphs

The net mirrors described in chapter 5 will become an exciting and effective stimulus for e-commerce. Because broadband has not yet opened the floodgates for sophisticated digital expression, we have only seen hits so far of what will be gorgeous and compelling showcasing and advertising in digital media. Early Internet advertising did not establish a reputation for loveliness, to understate the pain inflicted by some of the banner ads. Things have already gotten better, but we await true expressive sophistication. The internal net relations that comprise digital expressive tools and web pages, plus the interactivity that the visitor brings to the marketing page are all new means to stimulate commerce when they are done well.

10. Epidemics Cascade across Nets

Malcolm Gladwell begins his book *The Tipping Point*[8] by recounting a commercial success that came about through the behavior of nets. It was the sudden, spontaneous reemergence of Hush Puppies as a fad fashion. The new science of sync investigates how a single event can set off a cascade like the jump in sales of the brushed-suede shoes from 30,000 to 430,000 in less than two years with no marketing or advertising. What will it mean for the likelihood of sales epidemics when every person has a handheld and is connected into the macro net? My guess is it will mean a lot. Perhaps there will soon be a major at business schools in net marketing theory.

DYNAMIC NETS GIVE US INTERACTIVITY AND MORE THAN JUST ACCESS

Buying something on the Internet can be essentially the same thing as buying an item from a mail-order catalog. E-commerce has done a thorough job of repositioning catalog-buying online. There are, however, two kinds of things going on when you make an online purchase from a merchant—the old kind and the new kind. If my favorite stores that sell red shirts now have online stores (which they all do), I can shop by going to one of those store's websites and finding a page that shows red shirts. I can then pick one out and very quickly place an order that will result in my new shirt appearing at my doorstep in a few days, or overnight if I choose. So far there is no difference between the paper catalog and the digital one online; the access to the shirt has been all there was. Dynamic, interactive online shopping will soon mean entering a alluring new global virtual mall, where you can compare, investigate, test, and try out from endless sources in endless combinations. The structure of the environment will be a pliable web of products, any one of which you can selected virtually and compare with all the rest. Thinking beyond my impulse toward red shirts, what about choosing a car? There will be virtual ways to test-drive competitive models. An interactive animation for that sort of thing will be powered by the new tools of network expression described in the next chapter.

NOTES

1. "Permission-based Mobile Marketing: Best Practices and Success Stories," White Paper, Air2Web.com. www.air2web.com/mobilemarketingwp_papers.jsp [accessed 3 April 2003].

2. Amy Harmon, "Requiem for a Cheerleader: Silicon Alley Magazine Is Dead," *The New York Times*, 8 October 2001.

3. "Libraries vs. Google: Competing with Google," *Computers in Libraries 2003*, www.infotoday.com/cil2003/friday.htm [accessed 24 May 2003].

4. Carrie A. Johnson, "Retailers: Prepare Your Site's Broadband Facelift," *WholeView TechStrategy, Brief Series*, 11 March 2003.

5. John Holland, *Hidden Order: How Adaptation Builds Complexity* (Reading, Mass.: Perseus, 1995), 1.

6. Steven Strogatz, *Sync: The Emerging Science of Spontaneous Order* (New York: Hyperion, 2003), 269.

7. Albert-László Barabási, *Linked* (Cambridge, Mass.: Perseus), 225.

8. Malcolm Gladwell, *The Tipping Point: How Little Things Can Make a Big Difference* (Boston: Little, Brown, 2000), 1.

5

NET MIRRORS: THE FABULOUS NEW MEDIUM OF EXPRESSION

> Now Moses kept the flock of Jethro his father in law, the priest of Midian: and he led the flock to the backside of the desert, and came to the mountain of God, even to Horeb. And the angel of the LORD appeared unto him in a flame of fire out of the midst of a bush: and he looked, and, behold, the bush burned with fire, and the bush was not consumed. And Moses said, I will now turn aside, and see this great sight, why the bush is not burnt. And when the LORD saw that he turned aside to see, God called unto him out of the midst of the bush, and said, Moses, Moses. And he said, Here am I.[1]
>
> —Exodus 3:1–4

Before you read further, look away from this page and inspect the burning bush in your mind. What color is it? Is it leafy or mainly dry sticks? Is it small—something perhaps a few inches in breadth, shooting flames upward? Or is it a large plant with only an internal fire? It is always fun to ask those questions of a group of children in a Sunday School class after they hear about the burning bush. They each come up with a different description of a personal, mentally mirrored bush prompted by the Bible's words catching fire in their imaginations. Although this chapter is an exploration of the expressive powers of nets—a subject you may think is of interest only to those who will create digital art—it sketches a crucial picture for anyone who consumes human expression as well. If you enjoy literature and the visual arts and still insist on using books to the exclusion of digital art interfaces, you are already missing a lot. Soon that will be increasingly true for performing arts as well. The expressive power of nets will be, very soon, second only to the human being in its teaching gifts—combining and/or replacing every other cognitive conveyance: print, writing, color, sound, motion, and all the rest. Acquiring knowledge will be achieved in an arena of human teachers, the nets that compose the subjects learned, the digital media that platform those subjects, and the minds of the teachers and learners engaged in the education taking place.

Before we move into the expressive marvels of the net medium, I want to make it perfectly clear that the net medium is not a competitor with the imaginative and cognitive powers of the human mind—albeit, the nets come closer than any other media to doing so. But every external medium is a lame knockoff of the magnificence of the mind. When you read a book, hear a poem, listen to a symphony, or view an artifact, you are experiencing the content of each and all of them in one of the supreme edifices we possess by being human: the theater of the mind. The meshed networks forming around us are becoming a virtual theater outside the mind causing exciting new possibilities for expression. I will not say the new experience replaces curling up with a good novel because a well-done novel counts on its reader supplying a lot of the story and setting. The account of Moses and the burning bush is far more meaningful when it is manifested in the theater of your mind, where the bush and its setting are woven from your unique set of memories and imaginations, than the depiction would be if it were painted by an artist, even a great one.

In an unfortunate disconnect, a lot of people dismiss the Internet by saying they would rather read a book. The choice between reading text on the Internet and reading a paper book is between interfaces, and not what the text has to say. Reading is a key way that we ignite into action stories within the theater of our mind. The ergonomics of reading from a CRT monitor screen leave a very great deal to be desired, especially when compared with the physical comfort that goes with relaxing in an easy chair with a book. The difference in comfort level is ergonomic—about how the body feels. If you have ever seen one of the original Gutenberg Bibles you will realize that the ergonomics of printing did not get off to a great start. A Gutenberg Bible held in the lap would quickly cut off circulation to the legs. The early printing fonts, based on the scripts scrawled in previous centuries with quill and ink, were not easy to read. Font designers have spent the last four hundred years shaping letters from which meaning could be most effectively grasped by flying eyes. My guess is that the computer you will hold in your hand before long will emulate all the ergonomic pleasantries of size and eye-friendliness of the paper book. In addition, it will be able to download any book ever written. It will also have interactive text. You might, for example, while reading Exodus be able to click on "Herob" to link to and display an illustrated web page describing the flora of the Mountains in Sinai. The book medium as a platform for the theater of the mind will stay with us and become technically more wonderful. Books of paper or of virtual substance are not competition, but complements, to the awesome new medium of digital nets. This multitalented new medium not only networks together every previous medium into a harmonic chorus, its synergy composes a radically new medium that mirrors meaning.

When I worked for several years as an advertising copywriter in the 1960s, I had a chance to try my hand at a variety of media. It was the Madison Avenue advertising golden times. My job was with the deBruyn agency in El Paso, which was home to three local television stations with production studios, increasing Mexican border trade, the booming national center of blue-jean manufacturing, and the birthplace of the Western-wear industry. My assignments included billboards for a bank, television spots for Old El Paso Mexican Food (then known as Mountain Pass), print ads for the back of *Western Horseman* magazine for Tony Lama cowboy boots, and newspaper ads for the Juarez Race Track. Not profound work, but my assignment was to convey meaning to consumers from the ads.

By far my favorite medium was radio because my cast of characters was without limit and the setting for the ads could be anywhere. It was fun. One series of spots illustrates what a radio writer can do. A small, drive-up-to-the-window milk outlet store bought a series of 20-second commercials. I wrote three spots that rotated in the time slots on the air. They each starred a different car: a sports car, a limousine, and a junker. A local announcer who liked to do voices came up with distinctive talk for the three cars: a snappy hipster chatter, a stuck-up flowing tone, and the crackling sound of an old guy. We were able in the brief air time of a spot to create mental pictures of three different character cars pulling up to the window and driving away delighted with their driver's healthy, low-price milk purchase. The cars did the talking and their color, shape, physical demeanor, and so on, were up to the listener.

There are a number of first-class websites devoted to radio drama. The term *"theater of the mind"* is often used for radio, although it is true that most any form of storytelling is acted out in the mind. The following is quoted from one of the radio sites and is written by Yuri Rasovsky, who identifies himself as "the nation's most distinguished unknown audio dramatist."

> Audio is the most intensely visual of media precisely because of its sightlessness. It doesn't lack visuals; the audience supplies them. The action takes place, not on some stage in front of the spectator, nor even in some space surrounding the spectator, but within the listeners' minds. The distinguishing task of the audio dramatist is to use sound, language, voice, and music to evoke and to suggest—to inspire the listener into becoming part of the theater troupe, into taking on the functions of scenic designer, lighting technician, costumer, make-up artist and special effects technician. No two listeners see the same audio play. The more the audio play stimulates images in the mind's eye, the more intense and personal the listening experience.
>
> Perhaps then I shouldn't speak of audio's special quality as "blindness," which suggests a limitation. It's the other dramatic media that are limited. Einsteinian physics proscribes them: mass, time, and space dictate the fictive realities one can effectively conjure up on the confines of a stage or within the borders of a screen. In contrast, audio, being incorporeal, has no boundaries of time or space, no limits.[2]

An anonymous quote on the site summarizes the thoughts: "The grandest theater in the world cannot match the one between our ears. Radio provides the players and the plot, the mind supplies the rest." These quotations describe the creative participation of the mind, which is being invited in new ways by digital nets. Radio dramas play out in the theater of the mind where, as Rasovsky says, there are not the limitations of the size of screen or stage or of time. Forming within the new nets is a virtual theater that is, primitively so far, a space with no boundaries of time or space. The new virtual theater is something of a sort that has never existed outside of the human mind. The virtual, digital theater performs within a thickening mesh of nets from which ideas and images can be reflected for the consumption and entertainment of you, me, and everybody. We are just beginning to glimpse this radically new medium of expression. The basic platform from which the new expression rises is nets of ideas taking shape in the meshed digital complexity. Net structure is a potent form of expression because it interfaces with the nets of the mind.

The theater in our mind provides profound pleasure throughout life. I certainly hope and expect that nothing in our arriving age of digital networks will subtract from those pleasures. There is nothing inherent in the newer setting to prohibit or inhibit reading, as I have said, a book or poem, nor listening to a symphony or looking at visual art. Quite the contrary is true. The networks will continue to bring us these delights, often in heightened quality. When I recall the radio signals by which I heard my first symphonies in the 1940s and compare them with what reaches my ears and soul when I listen to Beethoven through my twenty-first-century sound system, I know my debt in musical appreciation is very great already to digital progress. The network of relationships of melody, chord, and rhythm born in the wonderful webs of Beethoven's glorious musical mind is expressed to me through my headphones with exactness that would have only been possible during my analog childhood at a live concert, with a superb orchestra having a good night, playing in a hall where the acoustics were outstanding.

Our expressive formula gets richer when we realize that the symphony or concerto is itself a net, woven in a mind that is a net and played to the minds (nets) of the people in the audience. The science of spontaneous sync adds that the clapping response of the audience also arises from linking among webs of responders. The networked relations among the musicians and listeners affect the performance; the music is better with a responsive audience. The plot of a story is also a web of ideas forming a net, and the lesson of a parable is a net by the same definition. The structure of a painting from which the meaning arises is also a web work of color, shape, size, texture, and direction forming a net that speaks into the viewer's eyes. Ideas are also nets and the act of thinking is pretty much always a matter of linking things and discerning patterns. The biological platform for ideas and thinking—the brain—is also a staggeringly complex interconnection and meshing of networks. It is a logical supposition to propose that a virtual medium that can mirror networks will be the most effective medium we have to reflect ideas. There are several points from the list of things we know about networks that apply in interesting ways to the powers of expression now developing within the new network milieu and we will return to each of them.

Before going to the parts, it is crucial to realize that the sum of the parts is greater than the whole. We are learning in the new network science that the whole takes form through linking, both static and dynamic: expression is nets. The logic is very simple: We live in a networked reality, therefore we can most effectively express that reality in the medium of nets. The recent development of digital technologies and the Internet have suddenly given us a virtual networked medium for expression. It is a natural environment for ideas.

A single idea can be thought of as a discrete network. Whenever a different node within an idea is shifted to become the center of that idea, there is a new configuration of the net. Say you are thinking about a football game you are watching, centering on the quarterback who is in the pocket preparing to pass down field. Your idea of the situation configures itself around the guy cocking his arm to throw the ball. When he throws, your eye follows the pigskin briefly, then zooms to an end on the goal line. As the ball and three tackles rush toward the hapless fellow who hoped to make a touchdown, he has become the center of your thought's focus and around him everything else is configured. The network that is your mind gives you awesome abilities to interplay relationships. Omni-linking allows you to configure idea nuggets (nodes) in infinite different ways.

It is the pattern of a network of things that causes an idea. A mother, father, two sons, an aunt, and a grandmother are a family. The idea of family defines the relationships of the individuals. Expressive media, including language, use this pattern principle to convey ideas. A line with a couple of curves is serpentine because it echoes the shape of a serpent. Rudolf Arnheim explains that in expression "simplicity requires a correspondence in structure between meaning and tangible pattern. Gestalt psychologists call such structural correspondence 'isomorphism.' It is a requirement for design in the applied arts as well."[3] The challenge of expression is to interface the pattern of a subject to be expressed through a medium or combination of media. The family pattern is easy to represent on paper by using a family tree hierarchy. Interfacing the burning bush that Moses encountered is a lot tougher and may never be as well represented in a medium as it is in the theater of your mind.

It will be fascinating to watch the development of the virtual digital theater. The more direct interpretations and uses of media are also very important and are marching ahead powerfully in the digital, networked world. From the time fifteen millennia ago when a Spanish painter first applied mud and charcoal to his cave wall and scratched in hairy texture with a stick in combined media that expressed a bison, people have been using multimedia. At the cusp of the technological revolution, Leonardo da Vinci poked and prodded at the uniting of written and image-making expression and implemented his fifteenth-century version of multimedia. "Words alone, as Leonardo writes in the text surrounding his sketch of the heart and a lung, are absolutely incapable of describing what the eye has seen. . . . He found it necessary, instead, to 'draw and describe,' and the value of the text was in naming the parts of the body and describing them. These descriptions accompanied the drawings and conveyed the impressions of the observer with great accuracy."[4]

The key point of this chapter is that broadband virtuality—for example, of heart surgery—has almost reached, and perhaps now and then surpasses, expressing what Leonardo longed to be capable of capturing. It does far more in a different vein. Virtual surgery where tomorrow's surgeons train comes very close to what the eye can see and goes much further as an instructive piece, because the budding doctors can work interactively to practice their cutting and stitching.

It seems to me, although some will disagree, that digital media produce excellent virtual versions of just about every tool of the expressive endeavors. An argument about that subject goes in two directions. Down one path is the creative arts, where the physical crafts of applying paint, blowing a flute, flowing through a dance, and articulating artistry orally are sublime endeavors. Yes they are. I hope that as the Internet makes intellectual learning less cumbersome, more time will be allotted to children and young people to develop skills in all the arts. Among other useful outcomes, that would upgrade the artistic skills of those who ply the digital expressive trades.

The second path is toward doing digital expression well, and this one is important too—perhaps most important—because here is the primary place where communication of knowledge will soon be done. The initial tyranny of the tech guys in building digital tools and hooking up the Internet gave them license that is no longer justified to slap any sort of content they wanted to into the burgeoning networks. It is time for that to stop, completely. The network law of the few helps the junk to submerge as, for example, the one virtual heart surgery software that is the most accurate and effective will attract just about all of the cardio crowd, while the lesser interfaces will sink into obscurity. As the Internet matures, web pages of low expressive quality are slipping on their own out of prominence, or are barely getting noticed at all—because the power law rules the Internet. The great websites are to be found prominent and dominant at the high end of the curve of visitor frequency and the lousy stuff is somewhere far below in the long tail of the graph where there are very few page views.

It is not just the techies who have been guilty of relegating expression to second place. The "Skip Intro" phenomenon that proliferated in the early days of Flash did the same thing. Which comes first, chicken or egg? Idea or design? It is very tempting in Flash, and other powerful digital artist software, to begin building a cool movie and hope it ends up getting a message across. Another trap is to build all the great functionality underneath only to end up with a boring interface—or worse! The key to preventing either misfortune is to decide from the beginning what you are trying to say to the user: what does the client want to say? How can my digital project say it? Flash is at the edge of awesome future powers to help you say whatever you have in mind with several media: not just pictures, not just text, not just sound, not just motion, not just interaction—but a network, reflecting the structure of the idea itself that you are expressing. The network you create in a Flash movie can become a mirror of the network that comprises an idea. Websites themselves have always done that, although in primitive ways. Flash is the beginning of much more powerful network-based expressive tools.

When the many media and interfaces are fully integrated, the network they make up emits enormous new expressive potential. The structure of each of the following elements of an interface from the digital media is weblike—a net—from which the pattern of the parts—

nodes—to other parts expresses an idea. What arises is a gestalt of each and all these nets:

- the idea and other ideas that may be present
- a group of Web pages where the ideas are interfaced
- connections from those Web pages to sources within the global Internet
- the mind of the person who interfaces the idea
- the meshed nets which that mind sees and hears:
  - patterns of color
  - patterns of sound
  - the internal relations of the parts of each image
  - motion during time
- ideas arising from text into the theater of the person's mind
- the actions of the person interacting with the interface

The elements in this list compose a radically new expressive pallet. Its impact is going to be huge when we start using it more expertly, integrating it into completely new sorts of virtual artifacts. The new opportunities for expression are something like what set loose the Impressionist painting movement in the nineteenth century. The standard studio for oil painters had always been indoors with light cast from a single direction, through a north window. Their pigments were subdued because of the colored substances available, mostly mud and organics. The artists were essentially confined to their studios because they had to mix fresh colors every day stirring dry pigments into oil.

Two things changed. Brilliant pigments made from metals, the cadmiums, burst on the scene and metal paint tubes were invented that kept pigments mixed with oil fresh indefinitely. The painters quite suddenly could work outdoors. What they saw was bathed in light from every direction and their new vivid colors could be splashed across canvas like the beams of the sun reflecting from faces, buildings, flowers, and water. The Impressionists stepped into a sweet spot in time for visual expression.

I believe that today expression as a whole has moved—as the Impressionists did from the confines of a single room to the whole of outdoors. Expression has moved into the global arena of networks. There, expressive talent of today and tomorrow will ply the older crafts of color, line, shape, sound, movement, and the rest. They will also be using new tools made available by the networks within which the expression is embedded. My ideas for beginning to use what we know about networks to the ends of expression follow. Many of the characteristics of networks are listed in chapter 2. There are three for which I do not have comments. Perhaps you will see some connections. Network expression is a nascent craft and I hope my suggestions will spark your own ideas. There is much to try and much to learn.

TEN USEFUL THINGS WE CAN LEARN ABOUT THE NEW EXPRESSION FROM WHAT WE KNOW ABOUT NETWORKS

1. The Structure of a Network Is Not a Hierarchy

An organizational tree or hierarchy is a very limited expressive form unless, I suppose, you are painting a tree. Actually, hierarchy is a useful tool when manifested in descending tones of music and color, distinguishing the comparative importance of shapes and many other similar techniques. But at a deeper level than the notes and brush strokes, a work of expression is structurally not a hierarchy. Relationships within an image, story, musical piece, or concept (as we will discuss in the next chapter) are multidimensional, a web. There is a very good reason for this: Ideas are almost never hierarchies and just about always nets—and expression is always the conveyance of ideas. Long is the struggle to shoehorn webs of ideas into hierarchical outlines for the purposes of recording, communicating, and expressing them. Much of the richness of the ideas involved is lost and expressive gestalts virtually never arise. The digital nets of our new times readily cooperated to form themselves into a matrix that marvelously mirrors ideas that you embed.

2. Networks Are the Skeleton of Complexity

On the infinite canvas of the universe, the Great Master Painter created reality. We now know that at its most basic, the structure of reality is webbed—a grand network platforming the galaxies, gases, gravity, and the like. A network is nodes of something linked by relationships:

splashes of this and that whose relationships hold the pieces together to form some sort of whole. Our new digital meshed networks are a global canvas for a new medium of expression. There are nearly infinite patterns of pathways available to a message designer within the networks. These can be patterns of communication, commerce, investigation, and learning. A pattern can also express an idea.

I greatly admire the entry page of the Metropolitan Museum of Art.[5] It is a gorgeous piece of cognitive art from which radiates the idea of the deservedly dominant art museum. The expression is achieved by a harmony among these key pieces: a new work of art each day, a brief text about that art, the name of the museum at the top, a large background image echo of the edifice of the museum, a life-size galleries entry lapel button and a distinguished deep page color. The idea of the greatness of the museum is expressed by the synergy with power and beauty. The skeleton underlying the clarity of the message is made up of the links in the viewers' eyes and minds among the several parts of the page. The message becomes increasingly effective when a visitor clicks through more of the Met's Web pages, where a consistent color pallet and style of image presentation molds the expression into a larger statement in addition to the many smaller points made on the pages. The skeleton in the complexities of the website is the relationships of the links.

In 2002 Macromedia lifted digital construction to a new level by introducing a new skeleton-making tool. The term that Macromedia uses for what this tool accomplishes, *rich media,* describes it well. Their product, the MX Version 6 of Flash, combines text, still images, audio, video, animation, and interactivity. The files produced by Flash are called movies, but do many more things than what we are used to experiencing from film or television. Flash's more advanced function, and the future of the product, is the use of OOP [Object Oriented Programming]. Again, pulling way back to see the essentials, everything about Flash is nodes that are linked in various patterns. The Flash movie is a node that is made up of a smaller network of relationships among images, actions, and the like. Everything is digital in this complexity and the skeletons are networks. Furthermore, a Flash file can become the interface that sits atop an interactive functionality network that reaches out to servers virtually anywhere to draw data and send back information. Once again, the structure is networks. The expressive power of Flash exceeds that of any previous software and it is a net-making tool; it makes skeletons for expression within the complexity of the meshed nets that are defining our times.

3. Sync Emerges from Complexity with Webbed Connections

4. The Structure of a Network Is a Web That Supports Movement in All Directions

The sap of a tree rises in the spring and goes downward in the fall. Sap, which is a liquid, will act very differently than it does in its tree when it is released from the tree's hierarchy into a dynamic net where the directions it can go are determined by the web pattern of the net. The sap is no longer limited to rising from the roots of the tree or sinking back down. Exactly that same principle applies to how messages, ideas, and people can behave in either a hierarchy or an expressive net.

The freedom to move in every direction maximizes expression. If you will take a moment to think about a cat or dog you knew as a child, the node of that old furry friend will have links out in several directions within your mind. Perhaps you will be reminded of a back yard where you played or of your grandmother who also enjoyed the pet. Your thoughts can then move from the yard or grandmother in several directions, and perhaps even back along a different route of ideas to the pet you thought of in the first place. The digital nets are the most complete medium we have had in human experience into which we can embed networks of thought so that they are mirrored back virtually into an interface where we can explore them outside our heads. Of course we do that all the time in conversation, where the embedding medium is the person to whom we explain an idea. To some extent any story, painting, or dance is a reflection of idea relationships. Websites and Flash, however, are the most complex and efficacious nonhuman mirrors of thought we have yet experienced. They can form the reflections because like the ideas they interface, the digital nets are webs that can link in any direction. I think that from knowing that the more complex the brain is, the more complex are the thoughts it is capable of supporting, it is reasonable to extrapolate that the more complex the meshing of the Internet, communications network, and other nets, the more complex will become the dynamic nets we can enjoy reflected back from there. We are only beginning to see ideas expressed by nets, but what we already have turned a big corner into a new expressive era.

What I have been explaining is not just theoretical. It is already out there, although its appearance and effectiveness compared with what it will become are something like the difference between the Wright brothers' flying machine and the U.S. president's Air Force One. A sample of the state of the expressive net art, the colorful homepage of Disney.com is the main interface to a web with eight satellite nodes surrounding a ninth node in the center of the page. When your cursor passes over any of the nodes, a menu of choices opens. There is a hint of hierarchy in the stepping down to the second level of the website, but once you have done that, you can click and link in multiple directions. There are dozens, and perhaps hundreds, of links in the Disney site network among its pages and to other websites. The sum of a surfing experience around Disney.com is to receive impressions of the fun and action that the company is marketing. Your freedom to move in all kinds of directions strengthens the message that is expressed.

5. Nets Clarify Relationships and Let Us Experience Context

An expressive artifact—a novel, a poem, a play, a painting, a concerto, a dance—is a web of parts that become a whole. That artifact is generally independent of its context, although there are major exceptions, particularly in sculpture and architecture. There is, however, a valuable contribution that the new contextual powers offered by the Internet gives the expressive arts. Anyone with Internet access can quickly assemble the context of an artifact to do background and comparative studies. You can read just about any sonnet of note written in the English language at Sonnet Central (sonnets.org). At the same time you can read other sonnets by the same author and others in the same or different sonnet genres. If you have a favorite Rembrandt at the Hermitage, you can make a virtual visit to the museum in St. Petersburg where the canvas hangs. While the virtual painting is displayed on your monitor, you can open another window or two to wander through a web of visits to the Louvre, National Gallery, Prado, and Met to admire and compare other Rembrandts. Although both the sonnets and the Rembrandts could be experienced by flipping through books containing the works, the Internet lets you choose from just about everything instead of what someone else chose to put into a book. I predict that software will be created to make the selection and comparison process far less hierarchical and more netlike in the future. That will be a beautiful step forward.

6. A Common Type of Network Form Is into Small Worlds

7. Scale-Free Net Structure Elevates Winners in a Small-World Network

The law of the few that rules in the scale-free Internet promises that everyone who is connected to the meshed nets will get to experience the very best of the arts. This will work in two ways: geographically and by the rich-get-richer principle inherent in scale-free networks.

It is my great good fortune to be living the second half of my life within easy walking distance of the Metropolitan Museum of Art in New York City. I often indulge in spending time in the two rooms at the museum where many original Rembrandt paintings hang. For the first half of my life I never saw an original by the great master because I lived in places where there were none. When I visit the museum now, it is obvious from the consistent large crowds that even overcoming geographical distance may one day soon not be enough to enjoy the Rembrandts in person because attendance will have to be limited. Already on the Internet I can look at almost all the Rembrandts in the world. New digital expressive tools promise that the quality of these images will continue to get better and better.

The rich-get-richer or law-of-the-few rule within scale-free net structure promises prominence within the meshed nets to the best artifacts of all genres. When geography determined the art I could view and I was not in a large city with a great museum, I mainly could see lesser artists or very few top-flight works. Although I know of no investigations in this area, I would bet a lot that the greatest 20 percent of artifacts on the Internet are receiving at least 80 percent of the traffic. It is a little bit mysterious, but the cause is the nets.

8. Structural Nets and Functional Nets Are Not the Same

The expressive arts give a marvelous example of the difference between the networks of structure and those of function. The structure of the music an orchestra performs is set out in intricate detail as the notes on the pages resting on stands before the musicians. The functional networks fill the hall as the orchestra plays the piece. All the colors, lines, and shapes of structure in a painting sit in wait for the viewer in whose perception the functional network expresses its meaning. The superb new digital canvas receives the work of multimedia artists and awaits that of the interactive ones.

9. The Net Medium Richly Interfaces Gestalts and Isomorphs

There are many types of ground onto which we can place daubs of paint, runs of notes, or story events from which an expressive picture, melody, or tale—a gestalt—arises. Expression is achieved when the gestalt occurs; meaning in this instance is the same thing as the gestalt. Aha! is your response when a new gestalt is grasped: when you get the idea. In the next chapter we will explore going to the nets to get knowledge. So far the general perception of finding out something from the Internet is that you go there and read it, or look at picture, or listen to something, or interact with a tutorial that shows you how something works. All of that is correct, but there is more. We are not going to learn about the new possibilities in library science, which developed in an almost purely hierarchical world and is devoted to deciding to which shelf a book must be assigned. We will get little interest from industries that publish outlines and textbooks because they are very busy trying to shoehorn digitization into their ink-and-paper methods. Network ideas are a good place to turn for insight.

I think the key lesson from the networks is the striking structural similarity of a virtual net within the new network medium and a human idea it reflects. They are both gestalts: their whole is more than the sum of their parts. What I mean by that is not theoretical, although its manifestation is still primitive, as two examples show. You will get more, or at least something different, from virtually assembling a group of Rembrandts than from flipping back and forth among samples of his work chosen by others and printed in a book. Your idea of the Metropolitan Museum of Art will be crisper and probably more accurate from spending twenty minutes at its website than from spending an afternoon on the premises of the grand museum. In these instances, which of the two compared impressions is the better? I will not judge. The point is that from both virtual experiences arose meaning that became ideas; you did not just look something up in a book or ask someone a question. Your overall impression was a synergy of many things you saw and did while clicking through the pages. The medium of the future is the nets, and we are only beginning to use its expressive power.

10. Epidemics Cascade across Nets

DYNAMIC NETS GIVE US INTERACTIVITY AND MORE THAN JUST ACCESS

The dynamic nature of the meshed nets environment affects expression in several interesting ways. First, your clicking in and out, surfing, and looking things up are part of the expressive experience. This is a sort of dynamic expressiveness that is seldom found in the arts. You do experience architecture dynamically, as you walk through a building, but most arts are experienced passively. Second, in addition to mirroring the nodes and links of the ideas embedded in them, digital nets can also mirror the dynamic essence of thinking—thus surpassing old arts in this area. In a third vein, the dynamic talents of the nets provide avenues for self-expression as well as for the spectator. From your desktop today and your handheld tomorrow, the nets you create are dynamic and not passive. The difference is the same as listening to someone play a clarinet and playing it yourself. The difference is the same as watching a recreational video and hiking along the Appalachian Trail. A fourth expressive factor is the dynamic interaction among media. With each new medium added to the mix, the potential for expression increases.

Our Internet industry is barely beginning to implement the powers of interactivity. Again, the inertia against change holds us back. The step is not often made to engaging a website visitor because the gurus still focus on using a site rather than being there. But the crowd who view the Internet as a place to look something up will soon be washed away when the tipping point arrives from digital information to network expression.

NOTES

1. Exodus 3:1–4.
2. Yuri Rasovsky, *Radio Drama in the 21st Century—Yuh Gotta Be Kidding!* Radio College.org, www.radiocollege.org/rc/drama21.html [accessed 12 May 2003].
3. Rudolf Arnheim, *Art and Visual Perception* (Berkeley: University of California Press, 1974), 63.
4. Carlo Vecce, "Word and Image in Leonardo's Writings," *Leonardo da Vinci Master Draftsman* (New Haven, Conn.: Metropolitan Museum of Art and Yale University Press, 2003), 73.
5. Metropolitan Museum of Art, www.metmuseum.org [accessed 15 May 2003].

6

MATRIX NETS: THE NESTLING OF KNOWLEDGE INTO DIGITAL WEBS

Fig. 1. Optical photomicrographs in transmitted white light showing the representative Chichkan sphaeromorph acritarch imaged by AFM. (*A*) Specimen transected at its equatorial plane by, and exposed at the upper surface of the polished thin section, superimposed by a plot of an electron microprobe measurement showing that carbon is concentrated in and near its cell wall. (*B*) The lower half of the specimen, embedded in the chert matrix, showing the characteristic reticulate surface ornamentation of this taxon of Chichkan sphaeromorph.[1]

—Proceedings of the National Academy of Sciences

To grasp the nature of education in the aftermath of the Internet's arrival, our most crucial insight is to recognize the restructuring of ideas to be taught and learned. They have exited the artificial outlines and piecemeal texts of the past and are emerging within a unified virtual matrix that richly reflects the interconnections of the ideas themselves. The Internet is, as any perceptive person can see, chaos. We have seen in earlier chapters that such chaos allows for a new sort of order, which is something education desperately needs. Network science tells us that order can emerge from chaos. The emergence of the matrix nets—the spontaneous order of knowledge—is the defining phenomenon of the future of education. It is a beautiful thing.

When a nugget or network of human knowledge is embedded into it, the Internet shapes itself into a *matrix* for the knowledge. The chapter-opening quotation from a biological chemistry journal is describing the characteristics interfaced in chert (a flintlike rock) by a microscopic fossil of a creature that was alive 500 million years ago. Fossils are formed by minerals replacing organic material or receiving the imprint of the carcass of an animal or plant—in case of the journal description, a unicellular microscopic protist formed the fossil. In fossil lingo, a matrix is the material that takes the shape of the original. That is what digital nets do when you embed meaning into them. I watched that occur on a massive scale without the slightest expectation that it was going to happen. New network ideas explain what I saw. If you still think digital knowledge lives in linear branching trees that compose databases, you need to know that is not so: given a chance it will nestle into nets. I suppose the same is true of essentially all information filed digitally, but it is particularly powerful and elegant with the content of human ideas, because ideas are web structures that their digital receptacles reshape themselves to mirror.

From the earliest Internet days of excitement over the new information highway, people have made extravagant predictions that the Internet would become the greatest library imaginable. This would fulfill the dream of the library at Alexandria where ancient scholars hoped to collect a copy of every book in the world into the buildings by the Mediterranean Sea on the northern coast of Egypt. In the past decade, the part of that dream about all the books being in one place—a virtual one—has come close to completion. The Internet has, however, not become either a highway or a library. It is not a highway because you use it to be places, and you stay on the road that gets you there for as little time as possible. Competition is fierce to get visitors to a destination in a quick click or two. The Internet is a massive interchange—where some routes are circles and loops—hardly a thoroughfare. The Internet is not a library structurally, because a library is a hierarchy and the Internet is a web. It is only partially a library in terms of content. A library of the Alexandria sort is essentially a location for books and other learning materials of general and scholarly interest (at least for the purposes of this discussion) while the Internet has not only library-type contents but a very great deal more: commerce, communication, entertainment, and colossal archives of "knowledge" not of general interest belonging to everyone from enormous enterprises to individual people, the latter in the booming expansion of blogs.

What became of the Internet dream of the comprehensive library?

The news is good and getting better. The virtual library of Alexandria has already formed within the Internet, and dynamic nets can let anyone in the world through its entryways with increasing facility. The subject of this chapter is what happens to the books, learning materials, and other manifestations of what is known by humankind now that they are primarily located in the Internet. The quick answer to that is: general human knowledge is now more freely accessible, fresher, more cognitively powerful, and more available in context than has ever been possible. In a profoundly important unplanned change from the past, the digital meshed nets are forming a matrix that relates the ideas embedded into it in cognitive context.

In chapter 7 we will lament the failure of the education establishment to grasp this basic change. Before we go there, this chapter discusses some things we now know about networks, of which the Internet is a powerful new example, that explain the new way our species interfaces with what it knows. The substance of what is known has been absorbed by the nets, causing new structuring of its content that is quite wonderful—because it is true to the inherent meaning of the content.

I realize now that network theory has taught me that the fundamental thing to know about networks as a medium of thought and expression is that they virtually take the shape of the meaning they contain. Their potential web structure is restricted in no direction, so they can replicate every conceivable twist, turn, and relationship of a fact or idea. Think of wire frames used in animation that copy and assume the form of human dancers so the animators can paint the frames with virtual skin. Now think not just of replicating the surface of the dancer to create a two-dimensional surface; but think of the wire framing happening in three dimensions or omnidirections that thicken through the body of the virtual dancer. Now think about nuclear physics or the history of France being replicated in the same way. I watched that happen right in front of me and was astounded.

I discovered these surprising behaviors during my struggle to figure out the way what we were building was behaving as my staff and I embedded hundreds and then thousands of learning links into what was to become, to the best of my knowledge, the largest and most popular collection of study subjects on the Internet. As the collection grew, it began to shape itself in ways that I first found mysterious and have recently understood in terms of network theory. The meaning of the subjects we were inputting to the network was imposing its will on the shaping of the web form of our project. It took me a long time to figure out and to appreciate what I was watching because I grew up believing in hierarchies and snubbing the notion of interdisciplinary studies as intellectually compromising.

My conversion took place in several steps from the spring of 1998 until May 2001 as I headed a staff of Ph.D's and graduate students who scoured the burgeoning Internet for high-quality links in academic subject areas. These links were organized into context for the website known variously as HomeworkHeaven.com, NoSweat.com, and HomeworkCentral.com. In 2000 it became part of bigchalk.com and remained there until bigchalk was bought in 2003 by ProQuest, which folded the links we had collected into subscription products. As we built the site in the early days, we worked in rooms adjacent to the dotcom's business and technical space in the back of a small building on 33rd Street in Manhattan on the same block as the Empire State Building. Soon after we moved into our work area, I hung a sign over the entrance that read "We Are Content." Over my desk I hung an enlarged quotation from Stephen Jay Gould that read: "Like bureaucracy, knowledge has an inexorable tendency to ramify as it grows."[2] It took me about a year-and-a-half to realize that the words over my desk were wrong about knowledge, although they are undoubtedly quite true of bureaucracy.

The people I hired to collect the links were very intelligent and very knowledgeable in their subject areas. They loved the work. It was a relaxing change from the rigors of graduate studies—the Internet was new and cool and they enjoyed being perfectionists. We had scientists, historians, classicists, literary scholars, a linguist, mathematicians, and, briefly, an engineer and a lawyer. All were dedicated and careful scholars. They combed the Web for the best representations of what they knew and built and linked related sections. We learned that the only effective way to do this was to work from the inside out, starting with small subjects, augmenting them with other links until a small subject was comprehensively represented, and then linking that small collection to related (often more than one or several) small-subject collections. The process caused larger topics to emerge as clusters of the smaller related topics. As the weeks and months passed, the overall collection became quite massive. Slowly, we discovered something unexpected:

not a little, but a lot, of redundancy. The knowledge was not ramifying (branching); it was becoming a web.

The redundancy emerged by itself. It was not theoretical and not planned by the cohort of extremely bright people who collected the links. The redundancy was a natural outcome of the meaning within the structure we were building, but I did not understand why until three years later when I began reading about network theory. We were a bit dumbfounded by what was happening, as I suppose Stanley Milgram must have been when he stumbled on the six degrees of separation revealed in his 1960s sociology experiments. We were, in fact, observing outcome from the same structural fundamentals that were discovered in 1998 to explain Milgram's results. The discrete study subjects within what we call academics are not very separated and do not branch off into distant directions. Before learning about small-world networks, I thought of what I saw the academic subjects do as often running into each other and overlapping. The small-world parlance I have since learned refers to them as *clusters with connectors*.

We did not need the theory to pounce on the power of our emerging web. Although still limited by fairly narrow bands of delivery and the primitive pre-rich media interfacing of html, we went full speed ahead to locate comprehensive links for study subjects and to organize them from small topics that linked outward wherever invited by context. An example is the best way to illustrate what we were doing because the process is, as the books on network theory sigh fairly often, counterintuitive. You just do not expect what happens.

In a famous and visually familiar event, George Washington led the Continental Army across the rough and icy Delaware River on Christmas night in 1776. During the nearly six months since the Declaration of Independence had been signed, things had gone mostly badly for the new nation. After crossing the river on the night of December 25, Washington disembarked his forces at Johnson Ferry on the New Jersey side of the Delaware. At four o'clock in the morning they marched on Trenton, where they surprised and defeated the Hessian troops and turned the tide of the American Revolution. A section covering this event might be found in each of these books in a brick-and-mortar library:

A History of the American Revolution
A History of New Jersey

Military Tactics
Biography of George Washington
The Delaware River (History)
American Historical Painting

When I would research a topic like this one as an undergraduate in the 1950s at Northwestern University, I would spend some hours at Deering Library. My task would be to find a group of books like the six listed here. They would not be located side-by-side on the shelves, but would be scattered through the stacks. I would find them by locating the six topics in the long narrow drawers of the reference room card files, and then following the Dewey Decimal System number on the card until I found the correct shelf and then spotted the number on the spine of the book I had chosen from the card file. Interspersed with the shelves in stacks were study carrels. Once I had my pile of books in my arms I would settle into a carrel, read through the relevant chapter from each book, jot down points made in what I read, and copy out quotations for use in my report. My procedure was pre-Xerox and seems very primitive to younger generations. But what we watched happening in our work on 33rd Street was a far more basic transformation for research than the arrival of the copy machines—or even the initial arrival of the Internet.

What our scholars were doing in building the web of links called HomeworkCentral.com was virtually collecting into one place what I would have found in a chapter of each of the six books I gathered from scattered stacks into my carrel. The term I came up with for these virtual collections was a *packet*. I now realize that is not a good name for them because in the digital world *packet* means a bundle of broken-apart pieces of digital information that are whizzed separately through scattered communications connections and reassembled at their destination into their original form. We were doing something like what happens when digital information packets get where they are supposed to go and are put back together. The identification of these virtual assemblies as *packets* implies that they are going somewhere, but the opposite is true. They are, instead, elements containing meaning, which qualifies them to link as a group to other elements. In the case of our example, facts and ideas from the six book chapters together constitute a resource that contains the event of George Washington Crossing the Delaware

River. Our scholars would have collected six or more Web pages containing the same hunks of information scattered among my library books and put them together in what we would call a packet titled George Washington Crossing the Delaware.

As the Internet grew richer and richer in content during the late 1990s, it became possible to put together links to universities, laboratories, museums, library collections, individual scholars, and other sources to replicate not only what I would have found in the Deering Library, but much, much more. Sitting at a library carrel with six books had become a primitive way to do research. Among other, newer blessings, gone is the time-consuming chore of physically locating the books in the stacks.

Perhaps, like me, you do not have credentials to opine on the theories of chaos, emergence, complexity, and other areas of new sorts of science. I feel very qualified by observation to tell you that top-down library organization methods are severely limited compared with what networks offer. Dewey Decimal and LOC begin with large topics and work down from there, branching (ramifying) into smaller and smaller subjects. To find each of the six books listed earlier, I had to poke my way through the Deering stacks, moving down through six separate catalog subjects, something like this:

1. History > American History > States > New Jersey > Eighteenth Century >
2. History > American History > Wars > American Revolution > Battles > Trenton > Washington Crossing the Delaware
3. Technology > Military > Tactics > Troop Movements > Over Water > Washington Crossing the Delaware
4. Biography > American > George Washington > American Revolution > Crossing the Delaware
5. Geography > American > New Jersey > Rivers > Delaware River > History > Washington Crossing
6. Arts > Visual Arts > Painting > American > Historical Painting > Emanuel Leutze > Washington Crossing the Delaware

On 33rd Street we did not work in a top-down manner. We spread a web outward from each node (packet). Our American historian would spend a couple of hours collecting links about the events on the night of Christmas 1776. She might consult with our art expert who would undoubtedly suggest the Metropolitan Museum of Art's interactive tutorial on Leutze's familiar painting of the event that hangs in the American Wing of the Museum. The historian would place her completed packet of links about the general's river crossing into our American History online section in the eighteenth century. She would also link it to other events of the battle in Trenton to military history in the packets about water crossings (along with William the Conqueror crossing the Channel, Xerxes crossing the Hellespont, and the like), to the biography section on Washington, to Delaware River history, and to American painting. The effect was like going to Deering Library where I would be offered six entry points that would lead me through six different paths, all of which would take me to the same six books I wanted already assembled in one place. Of course the multiple copies of books required to accomplish that in a brick-and-mortar library would force the expansion of the Deering stacks to cover at the least all the city of Evanston, and more likely, all of Chicago.

Ramified means branched, and branches of knowledge are something that have long been accepted as natural and practical. Yet when we built HomeworkCentral, adding all of the so-called academic branches and connecting them on our website by each normal and regular cognitive association, what we came up with did not look anything like a tree. When our job was pretty well finished by the end of 2000, at least half the topics appeared at least twice, and many appeared three times or more, like my Washington Crossing the Delaware example. You could logically follow the links from several quite diverse entry points to arrive within the collection at the same group of links for a topic. Furthermore, a single topic unit of links could appear at different levels of importance depending on what other units were related to it in a particular context. Whatever was going on, ramifying or branching did not define it. I began to realize we had created a structure that mirrored the way academic subjects are interrelated in the mind by their meaning.

I mused and strained over the years we worked on it to come up with the right word to designate what we were creating. It was not a database, although a lot of people have continued to call it that, failing to notice the redundancy—which is such a natural environment for your mind as you use the collection for research that you are not aware of it. What the subjects themselves taught us on 33rd Street was that lists do not organize a cognitive subject. They pull it into pieces, as we will discuss in terms of education in chapter 7.

The word I finally settled on in my own mind while I was doing the work at HomeworkCentral, on what I now better understand to be a network, was *matrix*, in the sense of the word when it is used to describe a substance's relationship to a fossil. As described earlier, what a fossil's matrix does and the form it takes are determined by the fossil—by whatever the fossil is and how it was shaped. The meaning of the knowledge we were assembling was shaping the digital matrix into which we inserted it. The natural relationships were seldom lists. Few topics appeared only once, with relationships to only one other topic. Certainly books cannot act in these flexible ways when they are inserted into the shelves of Deering Library. In libraries the cataloging system shapes the shelves, which parallel lists and designate just one location for any particular book. Cataloging is more flexible, letting you look up a book by title, author, and subjects, but you still strive to place each book into a single physical location. Of course the cataloging system was initially shaped somewhat by the subjects it would contain, but that system is rigid and hierarchical. In the Dewey index, technology and applied sciences are in the 600s, and the 700s are the arts; they do not seem to me to be cognitive neighbors. In a more painful rigidity, library cataloging systems rein in redundancy. What I had labeled in my mind as our matrix grew free of hierarchy and top-down structure. Growing in this way the matrix became more than 50 percent redundant. These and other shape changes from the way we have organized knowledge in the past are all part of one phenomenon that I realized occurs because the knowledge has migrated from linear shelves into a virtual network.

An archaic meaning of the word *matrix* is uterus, derived from the root of *maternal*, meaning mother. The machines that have taken over the human world in the *Matrix* movies capture a nuance of the word in calling their incubator where humans form, essentially as brains in vats, "the Matrix." Reloading their matrix—a goal of the machine's architect—will allow their matrix/uterus to give birth to and nurture a new colony of deluded humans who live in a dreamworld and unknowingly generate the energy supply required for the machines to function. I realize my analogy may seem pretty far out, but it is not easy to recalibrate our perspective on the location and organization of human knowledge. In chapter 7 I present my view that it is extremely important that we recognize and act upon the fact that the primary location of human knowledge is now the nets. It is a dangerous dreamworld to occupy when you find yourself clipping knowledge into pieces to pigeonhole into a database—which is a digital repositioning of a list on paper. The real world of what is known by humankind is now within the meshed nets. It is accessed by dynamic nets.

The real-world matrix of human knowledge today, and for the foreseeable future, is the Internet. For the past decade, everything that is known has been cascading from every sort of analog platform—libraries, laboratories, museums, universities, expert minds—into digital files that have been absorbed into the Internet. I have told my version of that story in two previous books, which are listed in the endnotes.[3] They were both written before I encountered the ideas of network theory and acquired from there some new vocabulary and insights. In old words or new, the most important reality check for human knowledge in 2004 is to ask where it is located. There is only one answer that is not a deception: It's the nets.

Returning to the useful concepts listed in chapter 2 about networks, several of them tell us interesting and important things we can know about how knowledge responds to nets.

TEN USEFUL THINGS WE CAN LEARN ABOUT HOW KNOWLEDGE BEHAVES IN THE WEB ENVIRONMENT FROM WHAT WE KNOW ABOUT NETWORKS

1. The Structure of a Network Is Not a Hierarchy

Most of the subjects we think about are networks, composed of a web of concepts, facts, or plot. Academic subjects are not branches of knowledge; they are networks of ideas. Wherever you happen to be in your thoughts—in trigonometry, Renaissance arts, nanotechnology, grammar—you are pausing on a node in the center of links that reach outward according to the cognitive relationship of ideas; you connect out from where you are according to the underlying structure of the ideas themselves. Because there is this inherent structure, we can mirror this cognitive net online, allowing anyone who seeks to think about it to connect with a dynamic net to explore it.

This network characteristic of meaning is not something that needs to be contrived with regard to the development of what is known by humankind within the Internet. It is robustly spontaneous. An expert in molecular chemistry builds a website; the next thing she does is add links to other web pages that pertain to her expertise. Pages she connects to will also be nodes at a center of ideas that virtually link to others, thickening the web of molecular chemistry in the meshed nets. The Internet abounds in meta lists such as a page listing "chemistry links," but these lists are only adjunct to the fundamental way the juice of knowledge flows through the Internet. Clicking on a link in such a list is usually an effective way to jump out into a web of ideas. Most of the listed links will be nodes in a weblet somewhere that is focused on a particular micro subject. The flow of knowledge is not within hierarchies. It is the juice of a great and growing interconnected network of knowledge within the meshed nets of our digital age.

2. Networks Are the Skeleton of Complexity

The carcass of a lizard that lies in the right sort of chert for long enough (a few million years) will be replaced by a chert lizard of exactly the same shape and form as the creature that once was alive. Virtually speaking, the same replacement of shape and form can take place when a network skeleton interfaces the ideas of a lizard, but it happens a lot quicker. The fossil is physical and the digital network is cognitive. The range of potential for exploiting networks in interfacing complex subjects is too vast to even guess at. Network based media, like Flash, are already putting virtual cognitive flesh on complex entities and letting us interact with them. Animated history timelines provide the bones to give new muscle to relations among events. We are barely beginning to harness these new tools of insight.

3. Sync Emerges from Complexity with Webbed Connections

The scholars of sync date the first notice of the phenomenon to 1665 in the bedroom of Dutch intellectual Christiaan Huygens who observed the pendulums of two of his clocks synchronizing their swings. Perhaps I am seriously stretching things when I suppose we are seeing sync within the matrix nets of human ideas and knowledge. But I hope the sync sleuths will look for clues. Perhaps a fundamental aspect of the self-cleaning that takes place in network content is spontaneous synchronization. I described that as singularity of scale in an early book and now understand that it is the law of the few that makes the rich get richer. However, there is another way to look at that. When we let knowledge out of the tree branches of hierarchies and let natural-meaning matrices form, something happens in which the best of the insights virtually bundle and cooperate. I do not know if there is a mathematically explicable reason for that synchronization, but it is a wonderful thing.

What was I talking about? To get the flavor, go to Amazon.com to buy a book or WebMD.com to see what you can learn about your backache. Mention an author to Amazon or a symptom to WebMD and you will find yourself on a very relevant node, linked out in all directions to other pertinent nodes. The nodes in both instances are synchronized by their meaning. There are, of course, expert people at both Amazon and WebMD whose job it is to link books and illnesses by relationships of subject matter. This is the same thing the HomeworkCentral scholars did for academic subjects: all the polynomial pages together and all the pages about mollusks together. That synchronization was hands-on. There is also a much more spontaneous sync occurring when an expert on polynomials lists on his Web page other polynomial pages he admires and when the mollusk scientists interlink their Web pages. The latter phenomenon does fit the definition of spontaneous order rising from complexity.

4. The Structure of a Network Is a Web That Supports Movement in All Directions

To reflect the nets that occur as ideas within the human mind, the mirror must be as potentially complicated as the ideas themselves. The

Internet reached the tipping point to vast complexity in the middle 1990s. That in itself qualifies it as a strong platform for complexities of thought. There is a simple mechanical fact that is even more important: Within the Internet it is possible to hyperlink virtually everything to everything else. There are no rules of what goes where, just URL addresses for everything. The matrix, which forms fossil-like for any idea we embed in the meshed nets, has no theoretical limit to its ability to replicate every nuance and crevice of the meaning of the original. Ideas, which are native to the mind, can be cloned in the nets.

5. Nets Clarify Relationships and Let Us Experience Context

Again, the insight that is reinforced here is that the Internet is not just access. As we look at that in terms of what is known by humankind—ideas—it helps us realize that no idea is an island, certainly not in a network or your mind. The following concept described by Duncan Watts offers a glimpse into the magic of the network that is the mind:

> *The center emerges only as a consequent of the event itself.* This statement has tremendous implications for our understanding of networks. In a multitude of systems from economics to biology, events are driven not by any preexisting center but by the interactions of equals. [italics Watts's][4]

The center of something you are thinking about emerges from the event of thinking itself. Aha! you say to yourself, as things settle around a new nugget of insight. The context forms itself as the cushion of the node that is tying the current idea together. Even in an idea form as structured as the web of a syllogism, none of the terms has much meaning by itself. Each term—major, middle, and minor—contributes meaning from the context of where it sits in the statements and summary conclusion. The meaning that arises from the summary of the context is something different and more than any one piece a pattern can convey.

The meshed nets of the Internet, communication, and dynamically participating human minds has, very recently, given us a global context: Everything thinkable is becoming interlinked within the nets. That means that before long any nugget/node of knowledge will be found in universal context. If you access a favorite Rembrandt painting, it will be a click or two away from every other painting ever painted by the great master.

In discussing this point regarding expressive nets in the preceding chapter, I pointed out that an expressive artifact is usually its own context with little or no relation to the world around it. All the parts of a painting are inside the frame and everything you need to hear a symphony is the notes the composer has included. The opposite is true of most of what is known by humankind. We certainly learned at HomeworkCentral that academic subjects woof and warp among themselves, robustly weaving patterns of context.

As I have mentioned before, wherever you move within content, you are at the node at the center of the relevant context—at least that is so within your mind. When content migrates naturally into the Internet, the same thing happens. An example of that would be for all the best chemists to make web pages about their area of best expertise and then to link to other chemists' web pages that they respect. The context that would result is a stunning new gift to human learning and thinking from the nets.

6. A Common Type of Network Form Is into Small Worlds

We know from the experts that both the connectivity of the Internet and the neuron connectivity from which the mind arises are small-world type networks. It would seem to follow that the content of ideas mirrored back and forth from Internet to mind would also form small-world networks. I think they most probably are and expect the nets experts will demonstrate that one day. My assumption is based on the logic that if both containers are structured that way—that is both matrices in which the ideas nestle—then it would follow that the ideas that shape the matrices must also be small-world nets. Academic subjects, it would follow, are small worlds—arithmetic, algebra, geometry, calculus—interlinked into the greater hub of mathematics.

As I have described from our experience on 33rd Street, I have seen ideas jump out of the trees and cluster into the nets, as in the example of Washington's crossing of the Delaware River. What I have learned about small-world networks has changed my conception of academic subjects as often running into each other and overlapping. Instead, they form clusters with connectors. But then how does the same idea show up in several clusters? That is not mysterious—you do it yourself all the time. You are part of the world of the class you went to high school with, of the people where you work, and of the network of salespeople and fellow shoppers at the mall. Ideas, like people, can belong in a lot of places. The new network matrices of ideas richly replicate real cognitive relationships.

It is intriguing to realize that the ideas that create net matrixes and the matrixes themselves have no substance. Perhaps the minuscule burst of electron activity that supports a thought in a brain or on digital platform can be considered substance; even so, it is the pattern of relationships among the electrons that causes cognitive meaning. The idea of Washington's river crossing is a pattern of contributing ideas. That particular pattern of the river crossing is also a contributing piece to numerous other patterns: the life of Washington, the pace of the Revolution, the history of boats in war, and so on. Perhaps big and important ideas form clusters and become hubs—which I have, in fact, watched them do. They obeyed the 80/20 rule, as described in the next point.

7. Scale-Free Net Structure Elevates Winners in a Small-World Network

In the initial description of a scale-free network in chapter 2, I mentioned the results of the measurement of HomeworkCentral's traffic by study topic. About 20 percent of subjects got about 80 percent of the page views from visitors to the website. Network theory has an absolutely new way of understanding the ratio that occurred. In 2000, when these metrics were revealed, they became an excuse for people on the budgeting side of the business to say there was no justification for maintaining the 80 percent of the subjects that only 20 percent of the visitors used. My answer at the time was that the big pieces in the 20 percent needed the smaller pieces scattered through the 80 percent for context to enrich the meaning of the more popular subjects. I still make that argument, but network theory has sharpened and underscored the importance of not cutting the tail off of a power law curve. Perhaps those links less traveled in the metrics had been used as paths between worlds of thought; probably many were. Others were undoubtedly enriching for a few ideas studied by the many. Probably 80 percent of those who visited the subject of Washington crossing the Delaware were there to learn about it as an event in the American Revolution. The less queried link attached to the main topic that offered the Metropolitan Museum's painting tutorial[5] based on the event opened new ideas to the few who went there, enriching their concept of the crossing and of painting.

The relationship of the law of the few to the cognitive structure of ideas is a subject that will be interesting to study. For what it is worth, the HomeworkCentral metric in 2000 fit the pattern. It is likely that the meshed nets will increase their reflection of what is known, and my guess is that as that reflection becomes more complete and precise, the visiting of a few topics will dominate while many will be visited by just a few. Just about everyone will visit arithmetic (which got the most hits in the HomeworkCentral metrics). Only a few may stop by to study nematodes. In the small world of study topics, the nematodes will be separated by about six degrees from arithmetic.

An interesting and important side effect of the law of the few in the arriving world where students everywhere use the meshed nets as their source of study knowledge is they will be sharing the same common knowledge. A history student at Northwestern and a history student in Tokyo will literally be on the same page when they take a look at the Metropolitan Museum tutorial on the painting of George Washington Crossing the Delaware. As the law of the few tends to push the best pages for all subjects into prominence, new global generations will more and more be studying the most used pages in common.

8. Structural Nets and Functional Nets Are Not the Same

The phenomena described for expressive talents of networks in the previous chapter apply equally here.

9. The Net Medium Richly Interfaces Gestalts and Isomorphs

Again, the expressive talents of networks will continue with increasing power to interface compelling academic content.

10. Epidemics Cascade across Nets

The cascading across nets is a cousin of context. The openness of the nodes and links and their congregation at hubs that support the flow of an epidemic also make a wonderful platform for echoing the real-world relationships of ideas and events. Whereas our old enemy the hierarchy is seldom more than a simplistic abstraction of the real world, the complexity of a net can be a closely resembled reflection.

DYNAMIC NETS GIVE US INTERACTIVITY AND MORE THAN JUST ACCESS

> Nokia and the 3Rs: 6800 Messaging Device: full text panel, image rotates 90, phone, radio, MMS (multimedia messaging), plus: Converter II can do all that hard high-school-mathematics number crunching for you. It's especially useful when you travel. Change miles to kilometers, pounds to kilograms, or from your local currency to the currency of your next vacation paradise. Change temperatures from Fahrenheit to Celsius . . . or from Kelvin to Celsius when you're trying to grasp the niceties of astrophysics. Change troy ounces to grams, so you have a clue what the goldsmith is talking about. You can set your own conversions, too, in case you want to see how many doppelzentners are in a centumpondus. (By the way, it's 0.326, or 32.6 kilograms.)[6]

This text was found on Nokia.com in April 2003. It is the beginning of much more to come. To come are the rest of the 3Rs plus pointers and pathways to subject matter on the Internet.

Adding together the comprehensive content now in the meshed nets with the expressive talents of digital and network pallets, plus the interactivity of handheld devices that do the 3Rs and doppelzentners causes a transforming synergy for content. It all is platformed by the network matrix that forms as knowledge nestles into the digital webs.

NOTES

1. PNAS Online, "Atomic force microscopy of Precambrian microscopic fossils." June 27, 2002, http://www.pnas.org/cgi/content/full/99/14/9117 [accessed 16 May 2003].

2. Lynn Margulis and Karlene V. Schwartz, *Five Kingdoms, An Illustrated Guide to the Phyla of Life on Earth*, Foreword by Stephen Jay Gould (New York: W.H. Freeman and Company, 1998) xi.

3. Judy Breck, *The Wireless Age: Its Meaning for Learning and Schools* and *How We Will Learn in the 21st Century* (Lanham, Md.: Scarecrow Education, 2001 and 2002).

4. Duncan J. Watts, *Six Degrees: The Science of a Connected Age.* (New York: W.W. Norton, 2003), 53.

5. Metropolitan Museum of Art, metmuseum.org/explore/gw/el_gw.htm [accessed 20 May 2003].

6. Nokia.com, www.nokia.com/madaboutwriting/main.html [accessed 18 April 2003].

7

A NET FULL OF INSECTS: HOW NETWORKS EXPLAIN EGREGIOUS EDUCATION ERRORS

> All too much learning is still like a net full of insects. What some teachers have collected in their nets is numbers, dates, lists of famous persons, lists of events. But to children, the world does not look like that. When their eyes explore the world, they see happenings, people, and things acting upon each other. There is attraction and repulsion, helping and fighting, mutual influence in innumerable ways. This is what children see, and this is what they need to learn about. . . . In education we have been burdened by a tradition that separates perceiving and thinking, as though they were entirely different activities."[1]
>
> —Rudolph Arnheim

Please be forewarned: this chapter is very negative concerning the established ways we educate our children. It is in no way intended to be unappreciative of the wonderful people inside the system who give their all to educate kids in spite of the often grossly dysfunctional schools in which they find themselves. I have been candid in the face of what I believe is the disaster of education because I think network science is showing us a far better way to give our kids the knowledge we all want them to have. That said, we move on to examine the net full of insects.

From three major perspectives, the new network theory explains sweeping fundamental flaws in the way we try to educate our children. First, the education establishment has largely taken over the wiring of schools as a means of implementing and repositioning its usual ways of doing things without taking advantage of new opportunities to enhance learning inherent in networks. Second, our kids are increasingly experiencing the stimulation of the digital meshed webs outside of school, making analog isolation in classrooms an ever-worsening imprisonment of boredom and irrelevancy. Third, schools flagrantly violate the rules of networking by serving up nets full of insects called curricula and standards instead of weaving webs of knowledge and thought—with the result of stunting learning and turning off minds.

The great wiring takeover in schools was a perfectly natural reaction to a new medium. The corporations did the same thing with their early websites when they interfaced their hierarchy of corporate organization as the schematic layout and navigation of their sites. This trend is still a problem, but the competitive world caught on and changed quickly when it realized the bottom line was affected by not pleasing website visitors. To the extent that schools use their wiring for administrative functions, they are doing little more than upgrading from a ditto machine to a Xerox: it works better but does the same job. The great promise that wiring the schools would put students in touch with learning has come true only in a minor way in wired schools—where among other problems, the computers are not portable, tend to breakdown, and are a technical mystery to most old-line educators. The arrival into the hands of the students and teachers of mobile Internet access will create an entirely different mix. The change will be from a hierarchical, top-down process through a tree of wires to a dynamic network spreading among teachers, students, and online resources. This will free the resources to become more prominent in the study mix than they are in an environment of wired instructions and control.

On the second point, that our kids are more dynamic and connected than what they experience in school, their misfit to old-way learning environments is becoming more and more obvious. The following from a quotation in chapter 2 bears repeating. It is a key observation about kids by Frank Newman, former president of the Education Commission of the States and current director of the Futures Project at Brown University.

> The most important concern for educators today is the 12-year-old who, in about 6 years, is going to enter a college or university. If you spend any

> time with 12-year-olds, you will discover that they spend a lot of time with technology, but they use it in a different way than we do. In a recent communication, John Seely Brown said that people keep talking about students being technologically literate but that, to 12-year-olds, technology literacy is not the main concern. What matters to them is that technology is how you talk to people, how you meet people, and how you deal with people. They play computer games that feature fabulous simulation. They learn intuitively. We, on the other hand, are text-based learners. If we want someone to learn a concept, then we ask him or her to read the following 270 pages and be prepared for a discussion of the text during the next class. That is not how today's 12-year-olds learn; in fact, it is not how they do anything. They plunge right in, and they are very successful when they do so.[2]

Kids cast nets that are *dynamic* and they are usually better at deploying and benefiting from dynamic nets than the adults are. If that gets us to wondering why, we will have begun a crucial reevaluation.

The time is very, very much overdue for us to step back and take a look at how we prepare our children to deal with academic knowledge in a transitional world that will soon be barely recognizable from the one in which any adult grew up. There is no cosmic cookie-cutter that stamped civilization with an education system with school buildings, textbooks, grade separations, curriculum standards, isolation from productivity in the economy, and senior proms. Quite the opposite is true. Our species has tried lots of formulas for nurturing children to adulthood, as anthropologist Karen L. Kramer discussed in *Human Nature* in a 2002 special issue on the topic of childhood:

> Notable in cross-cultural comparisons is the variable span of time between when children become economically self-sufficient and when they initiate their own reproductive careers. That variation is of interest because it shapes the age range of children reliant on others for support and the age range of children available to help out, which in turn affects the competing demands on parents to support multiple dependents of different ages.[3]

It is hard to imagine children delaying growing up any longer than they managed to do at the close of the twentieth century in the United

States. A hundred years earlier the majority of American children spent their summers working on farms, necessitating the three-month vacation from school that ten decades later is viewed more as a right to leisure. The level of academic content routinely taught in mid-1900s high school had become standard fare in colleges at the end of the century, and many college kids by then were taking a year off to stretch the undergraduate experience to five years. Childhood was no longer curtailed as one might expect among the economically disadvantaged. Women in their early teens began to have babies, but they were thought of and underwritten by their relatives and government as child-mothers, not as girls who had taken a defining step into the responsibilities of adulthood. Boys found surrogate cultures in gangs, usually ending the chance that they would become responsible grown-ups, or indeed grown-ups at all. A walk through the halls of a high school where demographics would assign the boys that populate the gangs will show that a lopsided percentage of the students are female; when you get to know the women you will discover many of them have children. A large number of the missing boys are in jail or dead.

One of the long-standing theories about why humans generally have twice as long a juvenile period as the next closest creature, the chimpanzee, is that we need those eighteen or so years of childhood to master the skills and knowledge to be a successful grown-up. Making that assumption today carries with it a fundamental contradiction now that the kids are far more competent with digital technology than their elders. Another article in the *Human Nature* issue cited earlier is about a study of the people of the isle of Mer in the Torres Straits near Australia where "children of crayon age were already dazzling with their spears and lines, and fully cognizant of the nuances of their marine ecosystem, bringing to mind an old Groucho Marx line: 'A child of 5 understands this. Fetch me a child of 5.'" That led the anthropologists to hypothecate that by extending childhood we keep the kids from being our competition:

> The new analysis of life on Mer,[4] where people stubbornly adhere to the ways of their ancestors, suggests to Dr. [Douglas] Bird and Dr. Bliege Bird that human childhood may not be what it so often is assumed to be: a built-in Little Red Schoolhouse, and a time when the young can master

> the many skills they will need to thrive as autonomous adults. Instead, the anthropologists propose that a long childhood exists on one end of the human life span mainly because a comparatively long old age exists on the other end, and that in a long-lived species there are benefits to slow growth that have little to do with learning—benefits like not threatening the older competition before said elders are safely stooped and toothless. . . .

Reading the conclusion proposed by the anthropologists, one cannot help but wonder if the longer we have pushed out our life expectancy, the longer we are willing to wait to let our kids grow up. I agree with this comment: "'It's a fantastic problem,' said Dr. Douglas Bird. 'It goes to the heart of who we are socially, our willingness to cooperate and provide and care for each other as no other species does.'"[5]

In another vein of comment about established education, there are other seldom spoken theories about why public schools are, as Jonathan Kozol so aptly labeled the tragic reality, replete with "savage inequalities."[6] A schoolteacher friend of mine in New Mexico whose students are mainly Hispanic children told me he is of the school of thought that the inequality among schools is simply how we maintain a class system in the United States. The racially incendiary bell-curve theory explains the imbalance by exploring indications that on an overall average blacks are not as intelligent as other genetic groups. The authors point out with candor and accuracy how we weave and warp ideas in this very difficult area:

> The dangers of the misinformation are compounded by the nature of the contemporary discussion of race. Just beneath the surface of American life, people talk about race in ways that bear little resemblance to the politically correct public discussion. Conducted in the workplace, dorm rooms, taverns, and country clubs, by people in every ethnic group, this dialogue is troubled and often accusatory. The underground conversation is not limited to a racist minority. It goes on everywhere, and we believe it is increasingly shaped by privately held beliefs about the implications of genetic differences that could not stand open inspection.[7]

It is embarrassing to suspect that we are maintaining a society that keeps its children in immaturity to delay their chance to compete with those of us who are older. It is sad to suspect that most people want to relegate others to lower classes or withhold learning because they belong to a race they deem not as intelligent as the dominant folks. There is yet a third factor that is probably sufficient unto itself to freeze our education pattern as an unreal world apart within the actuality of the twenty-first century. The vested interests of tenured school jobs, textbook profits, and having a system that baby-sits your kids while you are at work form and sustain an out-of-touch world into which people younger than eighteen are sentenced by law. The world in which our children are required to spend most of their time has become separate from the reality of our times, and it is getting worse.

The disquieting theme of the *Matrix* movies is the notion of not living in the real world, as this paragraph from the movie's website describes:

> Before breaking out of the Matrix, Neo's life was not what he thought it was. It was a lie. Morpheus described it as a "dreamworld," but unlike a dream, this world was not the creation of Neo's mind. The truth is more sinister: the world was a creation of the artificially intelligent computers that have taken over the Earth and have subjugated mankind in the process. These creatures have fed Neo a simulation that he couldn't possibly help but take as the real thing. What's worse, it isn't clear how any of us can know with certainty that we are not in a position similar to Neo before his "rebirth." Our ordinary confidence in our ability to reason and our natural tendency to trust the deliverances of our senses can both come to seem rather naive once we confront this possibility of deception.[8]

To be quite blunt, I say the schools are no longer the real world, and have not been for some time. The howls and screams from the education establishment to "save our schools" should be drowned by the rest of us with the demand to save our kids.

How do we save the kids? Where can their rebirth occur? Once again, it's the nets! First, end the analog isolation of every kid and, second, dump the nets full of insects into the meshed nets of context.

THINKING OUT OF THE SCHOOL BOX

At least two million Americans have taken their children out of the schools to teach them at home. There are nearly three thousand charter schools in the United States, each representing a group of people who have summoned the courage and wherewithal to follow through on their realization that there has to be a better way than what was going on in the schools of their experience. Some of the charter schools are hybrids that connect online to children studying their curricula at home. Fixing the schools has been at the top of the American and many other national agendas for decades. I am convinced that when every child has his or her own handheld connected to the meshed digital nets, there will be no need for what we have thought of as schools—at least not for the purpose of learning. Huge readjustments between kids, parents, and the workplace will be required to absorb the baby-sitting aspects of the current school system. The textbook industry will divide into companies that publish digitally and those that disappear down the same drain that swept away unnecessary dotcoms. The massive expenditures of governments and the school systems will dwindle and evaporate, and the economy will have to make a major adjustment. The kids will learn a great deal more and will be allowed to grow up.

What I am making is not a proposal but a prediction. The twelve-year-olds described by Dr. Newman are the first generation to have been born into the new era dominated by digital networks. They are, as Newman admonishes, different from twelve-year-olds of the past. They are already far down the road to linking up the structural communication webs that they will use for the rest of their lives. On a recent mid-afternoon I was sitting on a crowded bus going uptown on Madison Avenue in Manhattan. Sitting next to me was a small girl, no older than eleven, I would say. She was chatting with a friend standing next to her in the aisle, and said to her with some impatience: "Well, did you check your text messages?" Howard Rheingold goes into detail in his book *Smart Mobs* about the texting methods that have become the means by which people the age of my seatmate keep in touch and organize events. Cell phone use, if not texting, starts very young in the neighborhood where we were riding the bus. I was a bit startled not long ago to see, on the street in the same area, a woman lean down and hand a cell phone to a child in a stroller, who pressed it to her cheek and began chatting away.

One wonders what these youngsters will be doing by the time they are in college. Wireless network connections (now in place on more than half of America's college campuses) are shattering the foundations of campus classroom etiquette. A *New York Times* article in January 2003 sketched what the more than a dozen students in an American University classroom were doing who had their laptops open while a professor was lecturing.

> Many students went online to Blackboard.com, a website that stores course materials, and grabbed the day's handouts from the ether. But just as many students were off surfing. A young man looked at sports photos while a woman checked out baby photos that just arrived in her e-mailbox. The screens provide a silent commentary on the teacher's attention-grabbing skills. The moment he loses the thread, or fumbles with his own laptop to use its calculator, screens flip from classroom business to leisure. Students dash off e-mail notes and send instant messages. A young man who is chewing gum shows an amusing e-mail message to the woman next to him, and then switches over to read the online edition of *The Wall Street Journal*.[9]

The same article gives this insight from a recent report into what it will be like when the little girl who was texting next to me on the bus and the toddler who was talking on her cell phone are in college. "Although the study did not focus on wireless technology, the authors did delicately predict that 'issues readily apparent with the spread of cell phones, such as etiquette and distraction, are likely to emerge as students are able to access the Internet anywhere, including in classrooms.'"

As you have been reading, have you been wondering: what about the schools where those younger, highly connected kids already are? An almost comical sign of the times is the big backpack battle. The *New York Times* a week before the article about the professors' woes with student laptops ran a story about backpacks. Here is some flavor:

> On the first day of school last fall, Beth's mother, Carrie Anderson, weighed Beth's pack at 28 pounds, about 10 pounds heavier than the 15 percent of a child's body weight that orthopedists offer as a guideline.
>
> Ms. Anderson and other parents began to press authorities to act. Meanwhile, Ms. Hale's son Joel, who says he rides his bicycle to school each day carrying 42 pounds of books, was going through backpacks. "The

bottoms would just blow out of them, or the straps would rip off," he said. That is when Ms. Hale began her petition drive.[10]

A contributing factor in the heft of backpacks is the security concerns that have led to not providing students with lockers at school. But textbooks have also been gaining weight, as the same article reports: "Textbooks grew heavier over the past decade amid the zeal of the education reform movement, as officials imposed thousands of curriculum requirements on publishers, who in turn enlarged page sizes and jammed texts with photographs and graphics." The size of the American market for these tubby textbooks is an obese $2.7 billion.[11]

As I write this, Apple is advertising its portable iBook as "perfect for everything from doing your homework to playing games, and from watching DVD movies to burning your own music CDs, the 4.9-pound iBook fits in your backpack—and your life."[12] Dell is advertising a Latitude laptop weighing 3.7 pounds and equipped with full wireless connectivity. IBM's competitive notebook weighs 3.6 pounds. There is no text, photograph, or graphic that could be included in a textbook that could not be at least as well presented by one of these laptops. In fact, digital versions of textbooks are pedagogically more powerful than the printed page, with interactive text, moving as well as still photographs, and animated, interactive graphics—all of which can be kept fresh and up-to-date in real time. There is a downside—and I think a dark side—lurking in the $2.7 billion textbook market. It is awfully hard to bite the bullet and dismantle the hard-copy textbook industry. Profits, jobs, and influence will disappear in a lot of places. But until that happens, our children are carrying the burden literally on their backs when they should have packs with just their gym clothes, lunch, cell phone, and laptop. Within a year or two—if the foot-dragging in education stops—the laptop and cell phone will have merged and morphed into a student handheld connector to the digital meshed nets. The students will study material now imprisoned in textbooks by casting dynamic nets into the macro net of our digital era. The kids are ready. It is time for us to make that happen, and happily a lot of movement in that direction is under way.

History is full of surprises. The solution to the enormous effort of the 1990s to wire the schools that essentially was taken over for repositioning old methods is elegant. The wires are becoming as irrelevant as the old methods. Learning is now going wireless, but that is not the surprise. What we would not have expected is that networking children into the real digital world is freeing them from the isolation schools impose, and that wiring reinforced by fastening the computers to stationary locations. This isolation effected by the education system has separated young people from adults in American and European schools and the schools around the world that continue to preserve the remnants of colonial replicas. The isolation occurs as well in Islamic schools and in the way children are trained in many cultures. Perhaps the toddlers of Mer are expert ecologists because they are not excluded from the fishing beach. Kids learning from handhelds have broken themselves and what they are studying out of dictatorial learning hierarchies and set themselves free to explore the global web of common human knowledge. They are like the children in Mer, squatting on the beach at tide's edge observing living creatures.

There has been a lot of resistance to letting children and even teenagers use the Internet without supervision. I think a more realistic view of the future is to make sure we include within the meshed nets more materials that will benefit children, along with everything else that is out there. Censoring is a slippery slope and not to be tolerated, least of all as a guidance technique. A major failure of the education establishment concerning the Internet has been where it has protected its vested methods to require forty-two pounds of textbooks to the neglect of making the contents of the books available online—and in particular, online in context. That has slowed but not deterred the youngest generation from becoming natives of the nets. There has just been little useful material created for them online and they have been forced to spend time lugging and paging through great big books. As John Seely Brown and Frank Newman observed, "That is not how today's 12-year-olds learn."

People often ask me when I summon the courage to say out loud that I do not think schools work, what I would suggest to replace them. That is a bit like asking Henry Ford in 1896 what the Quadricycle he invented that year would look like in a decade or fifty years or a hundred. In 1896 he had put together something to sit on that had four bicycle-type wire wheels, the kind of tiller used on boats to steer and a gasoline engine that moved the vehicle forward at two different speeds. Most everything that was added in the next century was of minor importance in comparison with these basics. Nonetheless, in 1896, Henry Ford could not have described the Model-T that he would introduce in 1908, the Mustang that galloped on the scene in 1964, nor the Ford Focus that arrived at the end of the twentieth century. He probably felt pretty sure in his own mind as he rolled along atop his Quadricycle that it had replaced the horse and buggy, and that was the big change. The handheld connecting into the macro nets has replaced books and experts as the source for knowledge to study and learn. It took about fifty years to get most of the horses off the roads. The schools and books will be gone sooner.

What my guesses are for the future of education begin with a strong certainty that it will be necessary to start over with schooling, and perhaps not replace it at all. The home, child-care centers, and businesses will have bigger and more complete roles in nurturing children. Teachers of knowledge will become a profession once again and they will do their work both remotely online and in tutoring settings with one or a few children. The all-day classroom environment will disappear. Kids will be allowed and required to grow up sooner intellectually and in terms of productivity and responsibility for their bodies and minds. Apprenticeships will become important learning experiences and will make significant productive contributions to the economy. Children and teenagers will participate far more richly in articulation and the arts, spending much more time, writing, speaking, acting, singing, dancing, drawing, and painting. They will become explorers of academic disciplines, instead of spoon-fed. They will learn within the meshed context described in the next section. They will have time and incentive to become physically fit. They will know more, play more, and be happier.

MESHED CONTEXT

I do not agree with the opinion of many people who want to change the schools or disband them because they think traditional academic subjects are no longer important in the our new age of technology and digitization. Those subjects are certainly fading into the background, but that does not make them less crucial. The sciences, humanities, and arts are slipping into obscurity because they are being whacked at with a double-edged sword. The trendy idea that we should just teach youngsters to learn how to learn because they will have to keep learning new things as times change has become a wholesale excuse for not learning your history, chemistry, calculus, and Shakespeare. Meanwhile, the schools that agree with the importance of becoming competent in academics are, generally, presenting them to the new generation in nonconnected, undynamic ways that are indistinguishable from how their great-grandparents would have received them in a nineteenth-century classroom, except the textbooks are heavier and littered with small pieces of fact to match a set of standards somewhere.

The reality is that people who are going to have to keep learning new material are going to be far better at that challenge if they have already become competent in the disciplines upon which the new materials rest. A fellow is not going to become a very good digital biologist who does not thoroughly understand the anatomy of the cell. And if a budding biologist begrudges school time learning Chaucer, he should realize that there is no more effective method for acquiring learning skills than actually mastering a subject—any subject.

Another set of facts is being ignored by traditional pedagogues who do not use the dazzling new digital and interactive tools that make history, chemistry, calculus, Shakespeare, and the rest enormously more interesting than ever to interact with and learn. It is very, very hard for an adult to expect a five-year-old to grasp the principles of chemistry or the basis of the patriotism that ignited the American Revolution. It may well be that we are keeping her from doing it ever, because she is force-fed isolated pieces of it over many years until her mind has digested at best a boring jumble. To start toward a different approach, remember the crayon-age children of Mer who have mastered ecological nuances of their island and the toddler chatting on the cell phone. At school, and in most online teaching materials, a five-year-old child is allotted a portion of a subject that has been deemed by experts to be age-appropriate and which she is required to lodge in her head to meet a standard determined by another set of experts. We are so accustomed to this method that it is difficult to readjust our way of thinking about it. If children learned ecology that way on the beach at Mer, they would learn what a stone was at age five, a lot about fish at six, other animals like the octopus and crab at seven, spear-sharpening at eight, acquiring a full knowledge of their village industry somewhere in their teens. There are already compelling and comprehensive websites that present all of the aspects of beach ecology and industry—and chemistry and the American Revolution. Children are most often directed to age-appropriate online learning materials, like the hard-copy materials they reposition, where the cognitive content has been dissected and dumbed down. The Internet provides a virtual beach where children can experience knowledge in increasingly complete and compelling detail—as the kids of Mer do on their real beach.

The third network perspective mentioned at the beginning of this chapter casts new light on the pedagogical snares of what Rudolf Arnheim called serving up nets full of insects. Education today is a net full of insects and the kids are not biting. Grade separations, curricula, and standards are all responsible. Network theory is showing us what the error is—and it is a very big, bad error. Arnheim, who will be 100 years old in 2004, is the dean of gestalt aesthetics and not a tech guy. Beginning in the 1920s, Arnheim described the dynamic networking underlying the arts that the complexity and network theorists are now applying far more generally. He noticed from the expressive vantage point that among the scraps of ideas he calls insects in the earlier quotation, "there is attraction and repulsion, helping and fighting, mutual influence in innumerable ways." He says that is what the children see, and what we now know about networks tells us that they are watching a dynamic, not static, web. For decades we have been forcing students to catalog insects: "numbers, dates, lists of famous persons, lists of events," as Arnheim lists them. Those who have fought the battles for context have pretty well lost the wars of pedagogy and educational funding. Now we have on our hands a young generation that knows all about context because they have grown up with networking, interaction, and dynamic ideas. But at school, what they are required to learn is yanked one piece at a time out of its context and stuck into a standard.

There was one big thing that made Henry Ford's Quadricycle different enough from other vehicles to change everything. It was not the four wheels, which was the usual set up for most horse carts. It was not the tiller, a device borrowed from boats. It was the gasoline engine. One big thing will be at the root of the return to learning: networks will function in education by connecting everybody to everything learnable, and that will cause the key differences. Using learning resources online instead of giving every child a pile of heavy books will change school life a lot. But the really big change for learning when it is platformed within the macro meshed nets is that dynamic context automatically occurs. The insect becomes a node in a cognitive web embedded in a network of all that is known by humankind—and studied in common by all humankind. These wonderful factors that make the meshed nets a revolutionary learning environment marvel are not in the least contrived. They are the natural matrix interfacing that is caused by the web structure of networks.

As described in the previous chapter, we discovered that almost anywhere you were in the collection we had built at HomeworkCentral, you could move away from your location in many directions, moving toward any of several contexts. From the packet on George Washington Crossing the Delaware you could move away toward the study of painting, rivers, biography, military tactics, and the history of New Jersey or America. Try that on the page of a textbook! Visiting the George Washington Crossing node brings to mind an old favorite illustration of the expanding universe of big-bang fame as a loaf of raisin bread being baked in an oven. You, as an observer within the universe of that loaf, are sitting on one of the raisins. As the heat expands the loaf, all the other raisins in the dough appear to rush away from you. If you jump to any of the other raisins, all the others appear to be moving away from you, including the one on which you had just been sitting. Centers are always places of power and unique perceptions. The Model-T of learning will be, I believe in the very near future, the pedagogical gift of a handheld device placing the student who owns it always in the center of a network of bountiful context.

What will happen is marvelous. In a hierarchy you are always under things and over things. When you are at a node in a web, you are always at the center. In learning within a web you are in two centers! The first is your own position within your own understanding, in touch through some links with what you already know and reaching out through others to touch what you are ready to learn. The second center you are in is the content of what you are studying. Wherever you move within that content, you are at the node at the center of the relevant context. Although both centers are still primitive at this stage of development in cyberspace, they are becoming more and more precise and pristine as the Internet matures.

To many, that marvelous picture seems to be too much to expect kids to handle. The doubters believe it is important to be practical and make sure the kids do learn a few important things—things the experts see as important. That is where the insects raise welts. What we have learned about networks says that not supplying the connections may well be why students fail to learn even the minimum: what the links do is what we actually learn. The dynamic context is not only what catches their interest, it is what is necessary for the survival of ideas we want them to grasp. When a teacher prepares a study sheet online in which Internet links are inserted, if there is not a web of meaning apparent among the links in the lesson, and if those links do not offer other links for the topics they present, the teacher has created a net full of insects.

For many years my family owned eighty acres of land in the Lincoln National Forest in New Mexico. The Lincoln preserve is high country covered with pine trees and is best known as the birthplace of Smokey the Bear. Our property was in a V-shape canyon with ten fairly flat, tillable acres between two steep mountainsides covered with tall evergreens. The house we stayed in during summer vacations sat in the flat area away from the trees. My parents tried for several summers to transplant a small silver pine from the nearby forest into the front yard of the house only to return the following year to find that the little tree had died. I remember a conversation they had with a local cowboy about their frustrations. He explained that to be successful in replanting a silver pine you had to be certain it faced the sun at the same angle in the new location as it had in the forest. The little trees that died in the earlier summers had lost a crucial relationship. The pattern of links of soil and sun that interacted with their needles and roots to sustain and grow the tree broke down because the context of the sunlight was changed.

Removal from one's natural environment is fraught with danger. Think of a fish out of water, a jungle explorer trekking across Antarctica, or a redneck at a Boston social. Among the fascinating wake-up calls delivered by our newly networked digital age is that we have a very bad and deeply entrenched habit of removing ideas from the setting where they make sense—of examining, teaching, and learning them like a single tree with little regard for its native forest. The Internet is dramatically showing us the folly of our ways, and the arriving human connectivity of the handhelds will soon make the habit virtually impossible. An idea, like a baby silver pine, is part of a dynamic net of relationships that sustain the tree and through which the tree participates in sustaining other links and nodes near and far.

As I have pointed out elsewhere and often, the general opinion that the Internet is just another way to access knowledge is both wrong and a stumbling block to taking full advantage of the learning that can be done within the meshed nets. The education establishment has been a major player in perpetuating this misperception. The establishment has blocked students, especially in the younger grades, from entering the contextual Web materials with unchecked curiosity. Instead, the establishment has made an industry out of repositioning pre-Internet curricula and lesson plans online and then sticking disembodied pages into them to provide content to meet a current standard.

Here is eighth-grade Standard 8.1.1 from the state of Nebraska:

> Students will describe life in America before the 17th century by: Identifying and describing culture and economic systems of the first Americans, such as the Inuits (Eskimos), the Anasazi (cliff dwellers), the Northwest Indians (Kwakuitl), the Plains Indians, the Mound Builders, the Indians of the Eastern forest (Iroquois), the Incas, and the Mayans. Explaining how geography and climate influenced the way Native Americans lived.[13]

On a test at some point during their eighth-grade year, the students of Nebraska are forewarned that they need to be prepared to write a cogent description responding to this standard. Getting into the ninth grade is partially at stake. A Nebraska eighth-grader would have in her backpack a large social studies book with a section highlighting the Inuits, Anasazi, Kwakuitl, and the rest. The objective before taking the test would be to memorize enough of the facts in the textbook to respond to the question with facts such as: the Inuits built Igloos because it was cold and the Iroquois were intrepid squirrel hunters. From 1997 to 2001, when I worked every day building a contextual collection of Web links and packets into one big network through which a student could move from one idea to another, the pressure was incessant to replicate the idea of the textbook. A lot of big companies tried it—putting the standards online and then finding a link or two that related to each standard. Many companies have backed off from the process; others continue.

There is absolutely nothing wrong with Nebraska's Standard 8.1.1. It is a good subject and students will learn a lot from exploring it. The textbooks Nebraska uses may also do a fine job of providing information for the kids on all the ideas mentioned in the standard. When I was in high school fifty years ago, we learned things just this way. The textbook and what the teacher knew was about all we would expect to get in El Paso in the 1950s about seventeenth-century Native Americans—except from the Apache reservation a hundred miles away that some of us had visited. Today, however, the Internet overflows with thousands of Web pages that relate to subjects in Standard 8.1.1. You might jump into the Smithsonian's National Museum of the American Indian[14] website and from there trot about for an hour or two up to your virtual stirrups in rich ideas and images about Native Americans. If I were in the murky business of selecting Web links to attach to Standard 8.1.1, I would certainly want to include the Smithsonian. And there are many other excellent Native American sites. I would also have to include climate and geography Web sources and links to information about seventeenth-century culture and economics. I think the Iroquois were significant traders with the European settlers, so I would include links on that topic. To do justice to the standard, it would seem easier to connect to just about the whole Internet. Why, then, not do exactly that?

When the link collectors who work on standards just attach a few links to a subject like 8.1.1, they limit what the students learn to something like my textbook of the 1950s, which seems like a shame when there is so much more available. When they link to a lot more, the study of the standard turns into an exploration with many interesting byways that are not specific to the standard. In the final analysis, the standard becomes an insect in a net and not a node in a web. For the standard to be useful in testing students, it has to be sufficiently cut off to be specific enough to give the student a grade for his answer.

When the education establishment, with its highly developed skill at pulling concepts apart, encountered the Internet, which is a natural context-linker, there was a direct confrontation. Up to now, the education establishment has largely held off the Internet, at least below the college level. There are so many elements of the education establishment that depend on dissecting concepts that I doubt the establishment will be able to change. The grade-level system is a hierarchy of advancement that depends on learning pieces of subjects at different levels. Those subjects are treated as branches, which are from a pure form of hierarchy, the tree. In total contrast, ideas and the subjects they form are webs. You do not go up and down in learning the history of sixteenth-century America, except in time, which is no tree (except when the curriculum crowd makes it hierarchical so it can be learned in pieces).

Instead, to grasp history, you continue to connect more and more things you know into a network that spreads over the full time of the past, not some pieces. Grade advancement requires you to learn a few things each year in school, hopefully remembering enough about last year's facts to connect them to this year's. Because that does not happen very often, you tend to learn the same thing over and over, year after year until it is deadly dull. That is a network problem. We should not be threatened by how much little kids can learn. It is possible, for example, to teach a ten-year-old a very great deal about physics or Homer. If she gets the full picture of these subjects at one time she owns them as whole webs of ideas. The webs rise for her as the skeletons of comprehension from the complexities of history and literature. A net full of insects is not the same thing at all.

The collision of the education establishment with the meshed nets has been fatal for the education establishment, though it still slogs along. While holding off the meshed nets, the education establishment has essentially vacated its future function as a teaching institution. The schools linger as social institutions that beg to be replaced. The kids in school today are paying the cost of further delay in really changing how they learn. The action plan presented in the next chapter describes the key change needed: Provide every child with handheld interactive connection into the meshed nets. Learning is already well on its way in its own migration, following that of knowledge, into the Internet. There are a lot of good things about all this and among the best is that as ideas nestle into the nets they do so in cognitive context. Organized education has largely failed to grasp this change. Educators cling to the notion that it is they who do the organizing, but that is no longer true.

The meshed nets, like our minds, provide a matrix for webs, and webs are ideas. Curricula, lesson plans, and grade levels are clumsy platforms at best for a web, and thus for ideas. We learn from the new science of networks that the future of learning is the reflection of ideas from the matrix of the digital nets into the matrix of our mind. The fit is elegant. Only the exchange between the mind of a teacher and his student is more perfect, as Socrates well knew. Great teachers and their methods will be released from school strictures as children of the future spear the food of learning alongside their teachers at the real beach. The time is overdue for the textbook crowd and the dissectors of learning topics to gulp their virtual hemlock. It will make their demise more pleasant for them, and quicker, to the benefit of the kids.

TEN EGREGIOUS EDUCATION ESTABLISHMENT ERRORS IN NETWORK TERMS

The following highlights ways the new science of networks illuminates the failure of twentieth-century schooling. It also offers new methods and principles from what we have recently learned about networks that can guide the builders of the education in the future.

1. The Structure of a Network Is Not a Hierarchy

The errors of hierarchy pervade education. Networks offer a better structure. The essential structure of education now is hierarchical, enforcing the regimentation of knowledge and people. Administration is top-down. Control is top-down in the classroom from the teacher to the learner. Knowledge is viewed as branching, like a tree not a web. Students advance upward through a hierarchy of grade levels. Ideas and subjects are networks. All these hierarchies are called into question by the new science of networks. The hierarchies cannot be fixed. They need to be dissolved and removed.

2. Networks Are the Skeleton of Complexity

So-called academic subjects, which are named for the fact that they are studied in academies—schools—are not inherently organized in the simplistic outlines into which curriculum writers tend to shoehorn them. The new perspective the network theorists have given us of apprehending networks as skeletons within complexity is helpful. It is quite the opposite of conceptualizing a hierarchy (outline) into which to fit the nuggets of knowledge within a subject for the purpose of painting a big picture. The problem with that is the picture that emerges is usually not accurate.

Harvard professor of geology and zoology Stephen Jay Gould's 1989 best-seller titled *Wonderful Life*[15] tells the story of shoehorning the creatures of the Burgess Shale into just such an outline. The Burgess Shale, discovered by Smithsonian Institution director Charles Doolittle Walcott in 1909–1910, presented Walcott with a complex mass of 500-million-year-old fossils. He did not approach seeing order in the complexity but simply decided for each totally new sort of fossil he found to which established place in the tree of life it belonged. Walcott sketched trees to represent the rough phylogeny of the Burgess creatures by placing them all into preestablished spots on the tree of life conceptualized by biologists of his time. Gould wrote of the sketches, "They beautifully illustrate the restriction of ideology by iconography."[16]

The education industry justifies itself in large part by chopping up academic subjects and placing different parts at different and ascending levels on a hierarchy of grade level. We would do very well to re-think that process in light of what we have learned recently about networks. To isolate a few facts about a subject because they seem simple while the skeleton on which they hang is not introduced is like showing a Mer child a fish and a crab without letting him near the ocean. In the physical world including the ocean is hard to do with most subjects, but in the virtual world it is getting easier and easier. The education establishment should not busy itself with repositioning the disembodied simplifications but with introducing children early on to virtual representations of reality.

3. Sync Emerges from Complexity with Webbed Connections

In chapter 6, on the way content is formed in virtual matrices, we looked at how knowledge not confined to the tree branches of hierarchies tends to bond on the basis of its meaning so that the best of the insights virtually bundle and cooperate within the meshed nets. It is an egregious error to reach into this marvel with virtual scissors and clip out pieces to isolate into a lesson plan, curriculum, or grade standard. Figuratively, to use Rudolf Arnheim's metaphor, you will never hear a song of sync from a net full of insects, only from a hillside of fireflies interacting over their natural environment. If that sounds poetic and visionary, you can view a sample at the website *Journey North*,[17] which bundles the migrations of insects, birds, and other creatures who synchronize their migrations each year.

4. The Structure of a Network Is a Web That Supports Movement in All Directions

Of all the general principles that run through twentieth-century education, there is nothing more general than separation: separation of the child from the home to place her in a day care center and then a school through most of her waking hours; separation of children from each other by age; separation of children from the workplace; separation of knowledge into small hunks out of context into textbooks, curricula and standards. One of the outcries from the education establishment against homeschooling is that it delays the socialization of children. Network lessons teach that putting kids together mainly with others of their own age fails to allow natural linkages to extend in the many directions full socialization may require. Separating parts of a subject to be learned makes it more difficult to understand.

5. Nets Clarify Relationships and Let Us Experience Context

As set out here and in chapter 6, when academic content migrates into the meshed nets, it nestles into a matrix of its appropriate context. This serendipitous talent of ideas to be learned as they occupy the nets has not been encouraged by the education elite or establishment controlling high school and younger levels of learning. The senior scholars of subjects—professors, scientists, museum curators—have done a very fine job of webbing within their websites and outward to related links. The research of professional scholars and university level students have, as a result, moved almost completely into the meshed nets. The time is long overdue for the younger students to do the same. Expecting them to learn one fish and tri-cornered hat at a time is unrealistic and the root of their boredom.

6. A Common Type of Network Form Is into Small Worlds

Arranging study subjects into artificial structures of standards, curricula, and grades prevents them from being studied in relationships of the network that is naturally patterned by the ideas that compose them. Intuitively, the relationships among many subjects feel like small worlds, although I have no authority or science to back that up. There seems to be within the overall sciences a cluster of physics, one of chemistry, others of biology and earth sciences. The same is true of humanities, with the different worlds of literature, for example: British, American, French, Chinese, Arabian, Indian, and on and on. These all interconnect in many ways.

Few idea nuggets are likely to be separated by more than a few degrees. Many seem to be redundant, like plots of stories that appear in many different cultures. I am certain that the future of academics includes a lot of fascinating investigation and revolutionary discoveries as network theory is used to investigate the structure and organization of knowledge in terms of its meaning. I realize that digital knowledge management is an enormous field encompassing the huge database resources that populate intranets and the Internet. The academic subjects as interconnecting small worlds unto themselves is a network study and not a database matter because a database is a hierarchy, not a network—a tree, not a web.

7. Scale-Free Net Structure Elevates Winners in a Small-World Network

The education establishment has long supported competition among textbook and other suppliers to provide the best version of study materials for topics included in school curricula. A key factor that made this work was the geographical scattering of schools and the huge expenditures of districts and states for the books and materials to provide to their students. The students consumed the materials, wearing out books, most of which became obsolete anyway. The incredible economy of online knowledge cuts this whole process off at the ankles. In the new way things are, instead of the books going to the students, the students should be connecting virtually to the knowledge. Every student on the planet can, at least theoretically, connect to a single source for a piece of knowledge. One interactive periodic table of elements is actually all that is needed. Why shouldn't everybody use the best one? What the network theorists call the law of the few should and will apply in the future. The best interactive multiplication tables tutorial, the best reproductions of Rembrandt's paintings, the most cogent animation of mitosis, the best images of recent volcano eruptions—all digital knowledge avatars can now be used in common by every learner on earth. As soon as we make the transition happen, they will hold them in their hands.

8. Structural Nets and Functional Nets Are Not the Same

A subject standard like Nebraska's 8.1.1 discussed earlier presents a web of relations among tribes and of them to weather and the climate. This sort of project is hailed in pedagogy as an exercise that develops critical thinking because students need to make the connections among the pieces that are listed in the assignment. The network theorists make an important new distinction between two ways nodes are linked: by structure and by function, the latter being dynamic. Repeating Barabási's quote on this point in chapter 1: "Recently, however, scientists have discovered that genes also play an important *functional* role as members of a complex cellular network. This functional role is apparent only in the dynamic context in which an individual gene interacts with many other cellular components."[18]

My guess is that a pat set of relationships available in a textbook to give a student enough to respond to a standard like 8.1.1 becomes structural and not dynamic. Exploring the subjects in Standard 8.1.1 on the Internet quickly becomes dynamic, both in the clicking from page to page and site to site and in the explorer's thinking. To the extent that the experience is dynamic it would spark the function of thinking—seeing and grasping new linkages. Although that would be a very ineffective way to study to be tested for Standard 8.1.1, it would be a very good way to learn something about seventeenth-century American history.

9. The Net Medium Richly Interfaces Gestalts and Isomorphs

To combine the new expressive tools described in chapter 5 with the migration of what is known by humankind into the meshed nets described in chapter 6 is to bring online a new and magnificent learning environment. As I was working on this chapter about the errors in education revealed by understanding networks, *Nature* announced that shooting digital monsters is good for kids. The *New York Times* put it on the front page:

> And now, the news that every parent dreads. Researchers are reporting today that first-person-shooter video games—the kind that require players to kill or maim enemies or monsters that pop out of nowhere—sharply improve visual attention skills. Experienced players of these games are 30 percent to 50 percent better than nonplayers at taking in everything that happens around them, according to the research, which appears today in the journal *Nature*. They identify objects in their peripheral vision, perceiving numerous objects without having to count them, switch attention rapidly and track many items at once. Nor are players simply faster at these tasks, said Dr. Daphne Bavelier, an associate professor of cognitive neuroscience at the University of Rochester, who led the study. First-person action games increase the brain's capacity to spread attention over a wide range of events.[19]

Whatever the intentions, the kids who use the shoot-em-up video games do sharpen their visual and mental skills. The education establishment has not made a significant effort to use the expressive powers of the new digital media below the university level. Surgeons in training who operate on isomorphs of organs are, like kids killing virtual monsters, honing their skills. The difference is that the surgeons are learning to heal people and the kids are doing the opposite, at least in the instance reported in *Nature*.

10. Epidemics Cascade across Nets

To their credit, the education establishment—at least a lot of teachers around the systems—have established networking with other classes in distant towns and countries. The *Journey North* migration website mentioned above is an example of students connecting to and through projects online. Coming from the cell phone side, kids are networking among themselves at exponentially increasing rates. As the great global hook-up continues and thickens, the potential for cascading epidemics across the networks of students (kids) is approaching major tipping points. Optimist that I am, I expect some of the epidemics to contribute importantly to what the youngsters learn. The word could spread very rapidly, for example concerning a new laboratory website with cool graphics. If you think I am overly optimistic, the 14-year-old who confessed in the focus group described below that there were times when he really wanted to learn something argues for my expectation. Kids often are bored when presented with knowledge by how it is presented. The handheld will offer more dazzling presentations than books, but more important, its owner will go there by choice.

DYNAMIC NETS GIVE US INTERACTIVITY AND MORE THAN JUST ACCESS

One day in 1999, I watched the tape of a focus group where the panel was made up of 14-year-old boys from a high-performing junior high school in Chicago. They were being questioned about comparisons they had made before the group met among online resources for learning subjects. The boys were being paid to participate and were very polite and cooperative. I do not recall much else about what I saw except for one comment that told it all. One of the boys was pushed several times for comments about finding some specific detail for a subject—physics, I think. He was clearly trying to please the questioner, but became impatient. Finally he blurted out, "If I really wanted to learn about it, I would go over there." It was very clear from what he said that there was a sharp distinction between resources he was forced to study in the school context and going about learning something for himself. The existence of that distinction is the most egregious error of the education establishment. Students with handhelds, who are the object of this book, will be in interactive, dynamic control of their own learning, and the error will be corrected.

NOTES

1. Rudolf Arnheim, *The Split and the Structure* (Berkeley: University of California Press, 1996), 113–14.
2. James L. Morrison and Frank Newman, "The Technology Revolution, an Interview with Frank Newman," *Vision, the Technology Source*, ts.mivu.org/default.asp?show=article&id=1003 [accessed 17 April 2003].
3. Karen L. Kramer, "Variation in Juvenile Dependence: Helping Behavior among Maya Children," *Human Nature: An Interdisciplinary Biosocial Perspective*, www.archaeoworld.com/journals/humanNature/articleDetail.cfm?articleNumber=231, 2 November 2002 [accessed 16 April 2003].
4. Kramer, "Variation in Juvenile Dependence."
5. Natalie Angier, "Why Childhood Lasts, and Lasts and Lasts," *New York Times*, 2 July 2002.
6. Jonathan Kozol, *Savage Inequalities: Children in America's Schools* (New York: Harper Perennial, 1992).
7. Richard J. Herrnstein and Charles Murray, *The Bell Curve: Intelligence and Class Structure in American Life* (New York: Free Press Paperbacks, 1996), 297.
8. "Brains in Vats and the Evil Demon," Matrixmovie.com, whatisthematrix.warnerbros.com/ [accessed 17 May 2003].
9. John Schwartz, "Professors Vie with Web for Class's Attention," New York Times Online, www.nytimes.com/2003/01/02/technology/02WIRE.html?pagewanted=print&position=top, 2 January 2003 [accessed 2 January 2003].
10. Sam Dillon, "Heft of Students' Backpacks Turns into Textbook Battle," New York Times Online, www.nytimes.com/2002/12/24/education/24BACK.html?pagewanted=print&position=top, 24 December 2002 [accessed 24 December 2002].
11. Dillon, "Heft of Students' Backpacks."
12. Apple Online Store, www.apple.com/ibook/ [accessed 26 May 2003].
13. Nebraska Curriculum Standards, ois.unomaha.edu:591/casweb/standhome.htm [accessed 27 May 2003].

14. National Museum of the American Indian, www.nmai.si.edu/ [accessed 27 May 2003].

15. Stephen Jay Gould, *Wonderful Life: The Burgess Shale and the Nature of History* (New York: W.W. Norton, 1989).

16. Gould, *Wonderful Life,* 267.

17. *Journey North,* www.learner.org/jnorth/ [accessed 30 May 2003].

18. Albert-László Barabási, *Linked* (Cambridge, Mass.: Perseus), 183.

19. Sandra Blakeslee, "Video-Game Killing Builds Visual Skills, Researchers Report," New York Times Online, www.nytimes.com/2003/05/29/science/29VIDE.html?fta=y [accessed 29 May 2003].

8

ACTION NETWORK: CAN YOU HEAR ME YET?

> The new thinking will also impact places where wireless penetration is conspicuously low—among real water lilies and frogs, ironically, in some of the most rural, remote parts of our world. A dirty little secret about 802.11b is that it can cover more than 20 kilometers with suitably directional antennas. Imagine reaching places that do not have sufficient commercial value to justify classic infrastructure. In these cases, the viral nature of unlicensed telecommunications becomes a major force of human development, transforming everything from education to entertainment, hospitals to hiring halls. And won't that make an astonishing splash.
>
> —Nicholas Negroponte[1]

When I was a child during World War II, we heard accounts of the Seabees, an energized force within the U.S. Navy that could build an airstrip overnight. These memories come to mind when I hear of it taking months or years to complete a construction project. Certainly, when a job needs getting done fast it is still possible to make it happen. The heroes who removed the remains of the World Trade Center from Ground Zero in less than a year lifted to the same beat as the Seabees. Our old enemy the hierarchy is the culprit in the numbing delays that afflict projects large and small in corporations, bureaucracies, and most any organization structured like a tree. Orders have to come from the top down and action has to move from the bottom up.

Part of a quicker way to get things to happen is the "go to it!" attitude of the Seabees and Ground Zero heroes. The water lilies and frogs mentioned in the chapter-opening quotation by MIT Media Laboratory founder Nicholas Negroponte illustrate another mechanism for effective action, which avoids the paralyzing hierarchy and ignites action. As Negroponte explains the idea: "Think of a pond with one water lily, then two, then four, then many overlapping, with their stems reaching into the Internet. (Credit for the water lily analogy goes to Alessandro Ovi, technology adviser to European Commission president Romano Prodi.) . . . Messages can hop peer-to-peer, leaping from lily to lily like frogs—the stems are not required."[2]

Exactly that is happening in two spots in rural Spain as described in this report posted on the Cisco website in December 2002:

> Initially, two pilot areas were selected: Somiedo in Asturias, a province in the northwest part of Spain, and Molina de Aragon, located approximately 100 miles east of Madrid . . . [to] enable affordable, cost-effective Internet access to remote areas. . . . The unique solution combined two emerging technologies in the form of the WI-FI (802.11b) wireless standard and broadband satellite (BBI) Internet access. Satlynx beams down a signal that is picked up by an antenna, with connections on the ground to multiple destinations provided by a Cisco Aironet 350 Series wireless solution. Broadband access is thus deliverable by Neo-Sky, working in conjunction with local authorities, to businesses equipped with a mixture of desktop and laptop clients. The Cisco Aironet solution enabled the delivery of Internet access to a wide range of destinations in each of the pilot areas, including the town hall, museums, libraries and schools.[3]

On April 22, 2003, a friend of mine who has been in the thick of the efforts in Washington and the international community for Afghanistan reconstruction gave me this candid assessment of the chances for connecting teachers and students in a country that is starting almost from zero in reestablishing education: "Judy, there is major problem with Internet connectivity in Iraq. I doubt an e-learning portal can make a big impact in the short run. Think about Afghanistan, there is still very minimal access after more than a year of reconstruction." His message raised the go-to-it! ghosts of the Seabees I remember from my childhood. They could have overnight bathed the land of Afghanistan with the Internet from satellites above or planted enough quick-growing lily pads to do the job on the ground. So can we. There can be big steps and small steps; all steps count.

If you are pondering why priority has not been put on providing connectivity in Afghanistan—and the entire planet—I think the answer is simply the utter newness of the idea. It is not on any list of what you do to restart a civilization or to terminate terror. The brand-new network science should be a wake-up call. It is time to focus on why digital connectivity is a marvelous virtual manifestation of the best of natural relations among human beings. No less than the fireflies of Malaysia, the pacemaker cells of our hearts, and the dynamic messages of our genes, for the best functioning of our global civilization, each individual should participate and be heard from within the complexity of humankind. We discovered about forty years ago that without trying we each are already only separated by about six degrees. Through the new digital connectivity of the twenty-first century we shall become separated by just one or two degrees. That will be a very new experience for humankind and one that network theory indicates will be quite wonderful—and natural, remembering the Oxford University textbook's bottom line: "Only recently have we realized that we reside in a world of networks. . . . 'Network' turns out to be a central notion in time. . . ."[4]

The potential acceptance of mobile connectivity within education is a chaos of paradoxes. The kids have been the first to adopt handheld mobility and a lot of people suspect they will use the devices to cheat at school. (Perhaps some will; some always have.) We have already looked at the $3 billion textbook business that is on a crash course into virtual oblivion. The past decade of wiring schools has in significant part been used to implement administration and control instead of learning, with the nervous insistence on firewalls to keep the children out of the main Internet. There is even a strain of concern that the digital divide gets worse if only some of the kids are connected, leading alarmists to advocate no connection at all. The day is long past for those who are in charge of education to see themselves as authorized to judge the Internet and its digital assets instead of using them. Not leading children into the magnificent knowledge in connective context now available online is the twenty-first century version of book-burning.

No overall plan is required to organize and implement the digital connectivity of all persons. Action is needed mainly at the node level—

making sure each person becomes a node in the human virtual web by interactive connection into the meshed nets. Doing that is eminently easy and practical. It would take very little, for example, to put lily pads into the village valley in the Hindu Kush and provide connectivity to the people mentioned in my parable of Abdul. That would be exactly the same as the project described above now in place in Spain. That would be doing what Negroponte explained as connecting "among real-water lilies and frogs, ironically, in some of the most rural, remote parts of our world." For Abdul's village, if the Internet cannot yet be grabbed in the valley by a satellite dish, the signal could be boosted in from as far as twenty kilometers away. Fifty laptops like those you see every day at Starbucks, or now in Somiedo, would then add all fifty villagers into the meshed nets. Within a year or two, far cheaper handhelds could replace those, by then obsolete, laptops.

The progress of this global hook-up will reach a point—how soon depends on us—when virtually everyone together will reflect a human web in which each person is equally valued and fundamentally free. It has been quite astonishing to me to become aware of this new adventure and vision that has emerged just now for our species. It looks as if the political ideals of my youth that yearned for a world government were fatally flawed by the inherent hierarchies of officials—as you see them portrayed now at the intergalactic level in the fiction of the future like *Star Trek* and *Star Wars*. Perhaps I now dream too far and too fast, but hooking up more people into the meshed nets is both surely worth a try and something that will inevitably occur. In the section that follows are my suggestions of the ways you can help.

If you find the notion that by simply connecting everyone things will work out well to be hard to accept and believe, here we return one more time to the 80/20 rule, which turns out to be a very old idea with a new name given to it by network science. It is found, no less, in an explanation of how things are by Jesus in what is known as the *Parable of the Sower*. The story instructs us that when the sower spreads his seeds, many do not become productive for various reasons: they fall where fowls of the air devour them, they fall on rock and cannot get moisture they need to survive, they fall among thorns and are choked. But there are those who "bear fruit an hundredfold."[5] The parable continues sketching a world that resonates with the recent revelations of network science:

> But that on the good ground are they, which in honest and good heart, have heard the word, keep it, and bring forth fruit with patience. No man, when he hath lighted a candle, covereth it with a vessel, or putteth it under a bed; but setteth it on a candlestick, that they which enter may see the light. For nothing is secret, that shall not be manifest; neither any thing hid, that shall not be known and come abroad. Take heed therefore how ye hear: for whosoever hath, to him shall be given; and whosoever hath not, from him shall be taken even that which he seemeth to have.[6]

When everyone can be heard, secrets cannot take root, and light reveals the works of those who would do terror. The parable also delivers the message that the most certain way for the 20 percent or so who will bring forth fruit with patience to have sway is for the seed to be sown everywhere and completely. The Good Book tells us that imbalanced contribution happens not only with peapods, but with people, too. I am convinced that is as good as it gets.

ACTION PROJECTS

The following is my list of projects that will contribute to the connecting of everyone on the planet. Some can be accomplished the fastest by the cooperation and action of large organizations. The militaries of countries could do a big and important job by beaming the Internet from satellites and relaying it into satellite dishes with WI-FI boosters on the ground. Agencies in charge of communications policies can set and achieve goals that enhance broadband and connectivity. The Internet industry can continue at full throttle to develop and produce increasingly effective and talented handheld devices. But one small company may do the job and become a big producer. There are important projects on the content side as well. There are good indications in network theory that as these projects gain steam they will sync, functioning together in a way that will quickly tip and cascade into full global participation—just like a hillside of fireflies and meadow of crickets! The following list is a general start that offers many places to begin completing the network already well under way:

- Beam, upgrade, standardize, and spread broadband wireless access until it is available everywhere on the planet.
    - Complete ground and satellite coverage until the Internet is available to everyone on the planet via free broadband connectivity.
    - Upgrade, standardize, and spread WI-FI-type on-the-ground access everywhere on the planet.
- Complete development and distribution to everyone on Earth a cheap, mobile handheld device. The handheld becomes a person's telephone, pager, text message tool, information organizer, checkbook, and Internet browser. More uses will develop over time.
    - Accelerate the consolidation of smart phones and laptops into cheap, mobile handheld devices.
    - Sell or give a handheld to every person on the planet. Completion of this phase will involve speeding up technology and bringing prices down—but projects such as five hundred wireless laptops to key connectors like civil leaders and honor high school students in towns and tribes certainly are possible steps toward the goal right now.
- On every handheld, include interfaces for acquiring literacy and useful knowledge online.
    - Include a menu for online tutorials for the 3Rs; assemble and advertise the tutorials.
    - Include on the handhelds a menu for Internet jumpstart collections from which to choose one tailored to the locale and language of the person who receives the device; create and advertise the jumpstarts.
    - Include a menu for basic knowledge leading into pertinent websites.
- Enhance the knowledge assets for dynamic nets.
    - Continue to pursue network organization methods to replace database trees in libraries, archives, and so on with more network-friendly forms of organization.
    - Encourage and enlist the most knowledgeable people in linking their areas of expertise and enriching the patterns emerging from the process.
    - Establish collaboration of academic experts and the new

expressive net designers to speed up the creation of cognitive digital nuggets of useful knowledge.

- Unwire the schools and transform the school technology coordinator into the school network coordinator.
    - Establish WI-FI transmission in the vicinity of your school and in neighborhoods where students live.
    - Provide every student with a state-of-the-art wireless laptop and update these with smaller handhelds as they become available.
    - Revise technology staff into connectivity staff to build school Web pages that include knowledge links chosen by teachers for their academic subjects and a general interconnected cognitive resource for all academic subjects.

Every element listed in this plan is already developing spontaneously, and the dynamic nets we are currently able to use are the product of the synergy of these elements. As I complete this manuscript there are ads for wireless connectivity on television featuring a guy walking around talking into his handheld to see if he can connect to a signal. As he walks from here to there and talks into his device he repeats over and over: "Can you hear me now? Can you hear me now?" If you will listen carefully you can hear that question from every populated acre on earth: "Can you hear me yet?" Our world does not need to reel much longer, we just need to get everybody connected.

NOTES

1. Nicholas Negroponte, "Being Wireless," *WIRED*, www.wired.com/wired/archive/10.10/wireless.html, October 2002 [accessed 31 May 2003].
2. Negroponte, "Being Wireless."
3. Business Case: "Rural Spain Benefits from Radical Internet Solution," www.cisco.com/warp/public/cc/pd/witc/ao1200ap/prodlit/spab_bc.htm [accessed 2 June 2003].
4. S. N. Dorogovtsev and J. F. F. Mendes, *Evolution of Networks: From Biological Nets to the Internet and WWW* (Oxford: Oxford University Press, 2003).
5. Luke 8.
6. Luke 8.

INDEX

ABOUT THE AUTHOR

Judy Breck attended Texas public schools, primarily in El Paso, completed a political science major at Northwestern University, and received her bachelor of arts from the University of Texas at El Paso. After one year of teaching high school, she alternated for several years between writing advertising copy in El Paso and staffing Texas political election campaigns in Austin. In 1968, a job on the national staff of Richard Nixon's presidential campaign brought her to New York City, where she has remained.

From 1982 to 1991, she was coordinator of the MENTOR program, which established educational partnerships between public schools and law firms. After building the program in New York City, she facilitated its expansion nationwide. She also staffed six national Symposia on Partnerships in Education, sponsored by the White House to bring together people and projects striving to improve schools. Her concentration has been on Internet content since 1997, leading until 2001 the development of an online learning resource of 35,000 study topics. Breck is the author of two earlier books, *The Wireless Age* (ScarecrowEducation, 2001), and *How We Will Learn in the 21st Century* (ScarecrowEducation, 2002), both about Internet cognitive connectivity. She is also the creator of edclicks.com, showcasing knowledge readily available within the Internet and increasingly serving as the common learning resource around the globe. She is an advisor and contributor to the World Bank Development Gateway. In addition to her writing, she is a website developer and designer.

www.ingramcontent.com/pod-product-compliance
Ingram Content Group UK Ltd.
Pitfield, Milton Keynes, MK11 3LW, UK
UKHW041104150926
475561UK00001BA/31

9 781578 860401